M000166819

The Call of the Trance

THE FRENCH LIST

The Call of the Trance

CATHERINE CLÉMENT

Translated by Chris Turner

LONDON NEW YORK CALCUTTA

This volume is published through the Tagore Publication Assistance Programme, with support of Institut Français en Inde, Ambassade de France en Inde.

Seagull Books, 2014

First published in French as *L'Appel de la Transe* by Catherine Clément
© Editions Stock, 2011

First published in English translation by Seagull Books, 2014

ISBN   978 0 85742 190 6

British Library Cataloguing-in-Publication Data
A catalogue record for this book is available from the British Library.

Typeset by Seagull Books, Calcutta, India

Printed and bound by Maple Press, York, Pennsylvania, USA

To the memory of Claude Lévi-Strauss

Contents

Acknowledgements

Thanks are due to Jérôme Bonnafont, Jérôme Clément, Julien Clément and Jacqueline Laporte, my first readers and, especially, to Jean-Claude Milner for his many contributions to the writing of this book.

To Jean-Marc Roberts for his loyalty and Capucine Ruat for her kindly vigilance.

To Anne Dufourmantelle who was so kind as to accept these pages for the collection she edits and who has commented on them attentively.

To Ernest Pignon-Ernest for the cover illustration of the original French edition and to Anne-Christine Taylor for the dog Makanch.

To Tobie Nathan.

To Daniel Mesguich and the students of the Conservatoire National d'Art Dramatique.

And to A. L. as ever.

Changing Life

The scene takes place at Dakar at the turn of the twenty-first century. It's nightfall.

In a great arena of sand, beside the ocean, women are dancing in a state of trance, watched by a thousand onlookers. They make a majestic entrance, dressed in flounced dresses and lace. With turbaned heads and a flyswatter in one hand, they step out with joy and distinction to the rhythm of the drums.

They call the trance that possesses them 'dancing'. There are around fifty of them, mostly jobless, as are many of those who live in the Medina, far from the rich neighbourhoods. Unemployed or in minor precarious jobs of the kind known as 'informal work', the dancers have children to look after and ephemeral husbands. They belong to the global masses who live on less than two dollars a day. Women in poverty.

But when they are in a trance, each evening as night falls, these women are queens for two hours.

And we are too, sometimes. The trance is universal.

The trance doesn't come easily. You have to prompt it into being. Each of the women will go and lodge herself at the burning heart of the rhythm as a willing prisoner of the circle of drums—ten massive instruments wielded by griots. They're all men, men who 'bring down' women, including a young man armed with a little *tama* or talking drum that makes a buzzing sound. The women collapse on the sand; their fall is their genesis. To change our lives, we have to shatter them;

wherever we might be in the world, at a certain moment, either before or after, we have to fall from our 'high horses', and that's the rule for everyone.

Here they are on the sand, laid flat, unconscious. The drums essay different rhythms to find the one that will haunt their being. Now they have it! The women are coming out of their inertia. And when they stand, their spirits transform them. Into a crawling snake, into a chameleon that slowly rotates its heavy head, into a canoeist paddling on the sand, into a colonial soldier, blind drunk . . . Ten minutes and they fall back down. Then transform themselves for another ten exhausting minutes.

Elsewhere, the spirits are called djinns, angels, demons, devils, rock music, love, anger, madness or, quite simply, God. Here in the Dakar region, they're called *rab* and they come from the sea. Each spirit demands an acrobatic body, inhuman flexibility and stomach muscles of steel. This isn't without its dangers—it takes only a sharp pebble on the beach or legs getting caught in the long petticoats . . . or the sand grazing your chin. Without assistance, a trance can leave you with wounded flesh, broken bones or, worst of all, a damaged mind.

This is why some women are delegated each evening to deny their own spirits bodily entry and, instead, take care of the women who are in a trance. They remove the pebbles, smooth down the petticoats, wipe the sweat from brows and the foam from dry lips. They grit their teeth, fan themselves, puff and blow. Resisting spirits is no mean task. Ask the Christian exorcist—he knows. But solidarity imposes this genuine obligation; the woman who doesn't meet it will be excluded from the group.

While the attendants strive at their task, the others, the happy ones, paddle, stagger or crawl around silently, wordlessly, staring absently in front of them. They aren't there, they're elsewhere—in the depths of the waves. This is how these pious Muslim women honour their gods sprung from the ocean.

Muslims or polytheists? Believing there is no other God but God, as the Islamic creed has it, and yet honouring a little host of sea gods all the same?

Yes, both simultaneously. On the eve of the ritual, the trance-mistress, shut up in her bedroom, asks her husband for the Prophet's blessing on the ceremony. The very next day she'll oversee the emergence of the spirits.

In northern Ethiopia, in 1933, a Christian healer frequented by Michel Leiris was prey to *zar*, the equivalent of djinns. The old woman, a person of standing, had her explanation. In the beginning, Eve had thirty children whom God wished to count. Fearing His evil eye, Eve hid the fifteen handsomest. To punish her, God decreed they would remain hidden. Their distant descendants are the invisible *zar* that take possession of the visible human brothers.

Coexistence with the gods is commonplace today, the whole world over. It has very often been so; only human beings worry about it, not the gods.

Sometimes the spirits come of their own accord. That evening at Dakar, a cook from Mali fell down suddenly, without warning. Often mistreated by the trance-mistress, her boss, she wasn't one of the official group but among the onlookers. Yet the spirits are no respecters of class distinctions . . . A sudden jolt and off she went. She was on all fours, growling fiercely. The drums stopped. Among the griots, no one knew the rhythm of this particular spirit. A breakdown of control in the arena. Who was the intruder?

You could see anxiety in the cook's bulging eyes; they seemed to be calling out for help as she sought to pay due honour to a spirit not from these parts. The griots went back to work. They tried one rhythm on the drums, then another. To no avail. The cook roared so loudly that she was exhausted.

I saw her up-close. Her eyes, crazed with worry, rolled in all directions, while her breathing grew panicky and her mouth opened and roared involuntarily while her every limb trembled.

She was about to suffocate, perhaps even die . . . On and on it went! To bring her trance under control, the women attendants resorted to their usual methods. They blew up her nose, splashed water on her eyes, dabbed her chest with wet cloths and several of them fanned her at once. To no avail. At that point the roaring woman charged off into the crowd, attacking people. Her spirit was a Malian lion.

The leader of the griots, a brother of Youssou N'Dour and a man of some experience, had the idea of taming her. He called her 'lion' and reached out his fingers. She tried to bite them and he retreated. She followed on all fours, roaring even louder. He extracted her from the group, though not without difficulty, since at one point she ran off to hunt among the spectators, baring her teeth. Later I learnt how the cook stopped being a lion. It was done with raw meat. After she'd wolfed it down, they said, she fell into a deep sleep.

When I saw her the next day she had a broad smile on her face. In a voice hoarse from roaring, she confided to me that she felt rested. She was happy to have reconnected with her spirit. Without the rhythm that could be said to have calmed her? Yes. She felt rested as though after a refreshing bath.

Other 'dancers' used these same words. Rested, refreshing bath, delighted smile. Some stiffness . . . oh yes! But so happy from the exertion. 'I had a really good dance.' You'd think they'd just made love. You'd think they were just back from their holidays, they who didn't even know such things existed.

Holidays from life? For jobless women with families—African families that you have to serve in every which way when you're not a man, at any hour of the day and night, including when ten members of the clan suddenly arrive at four in the morning and you have to feed them because it's an obligation—trances and dancing in another body were clearly a holiday from life.

Or much more in fact. Permission to slip out of life, to 'eclipse themselves'.

We're all like these women. We all need dancing and breaks, times of silence and absence, withdrawals that may take the form of illness. We all need a sudden escape, a refreshing bath, a thrill that brings no lasting consequences, life without commitment or promise, disorder, holidays without beginning or end.

It may happen that your eclipse lasts for ever; that you never get over it; that you drop out of life. When you throw yourself from a high place we call it suicide. The danger does indeed exist. Eclipsing yourself from life isn't something you can do on your own. All alone, there's too great a risk. You need a caring context, the presence of an attentive group and vigilance.

These singular breaches, which everyone engages in, verge on death, their ultimate horizon. *Être transi*—the word that gives us trance—means nowadays to be chilled through with cold or fear. In the Middle Ages, it meant to be in one's death throes.

We're like those women when we make love, when we fall down blind drunk, when we fly into a fit of anger or when we think too much. And then we return. Something's changed and it's imperceptible; the mark of the eclipse brings a security.

The cook-lion had come back, she had got over it. She was calm and ready to resume work for her employer, the trance-mistress, who had been so afraid. That fear changed everything. You don't treat a lion-woman and a commonplace servant the same way. 'Such a good cook!' said the trance-mistress with newfound respect.

CHAPTER 1

The *Coup de foudre*

We have, in Europe, a 'licensed' form of trance.

In French, in an expression not found elsewhere, we call this lovers' trance a *coup de foudre*—a lightning strike. Love at first sight in English, *amor a primera vista* in Spanish and *Liebe auf den ersten Blick* in German evoke neither lightning nor a strike but refer simply to the first eye contact.

The French expression covers the key aspects since, in medical terms, the lightning that comes from the sky to strike a human being 'stuns' him by blocking his nerve centres. It 'tetanizes' him, contracting his respiratory muscles, and burns his skin. It can be lethal.

The symptoms of the lovers' *coup de foudre* don't destroy the organism as quickly but they're present nonetheless. You're thunderstruck, your brain paralysed and your breath snatched away. You're abstracted from the world—as a twosome. And flooded with joy, like that sense of fullness you get from delight in music, with 'the joy of the soul being invited for once to recognize itself in the body,' as Claude Lévi-Strauss tells us. There's an end to separation, all is merged into one. I am you, you are I. The 'we' no longer exists, and as for the self— what has that got to do with anything?

The lightning's struck and you've fallen in love, just as the African women fall into a trance when the drums give the signal—suddenly, wildly, as soon as you're aware of it. A vertiginous fall, followed by astonishment. To be astonished—French: *étonné*—is to be struck dumb by thunder—*tonnerre*. Once this brief moment of inertia is over, you jump back up and are light on your feet—dancing. You've moved outside of life. You're going to experience a moment of eclipse.

Your appetite's gone. What's the point of eating when you're eating with your eyes? You can't sleep. Why would you sleep when the nights are so beautiful? You don't drink enough water, you're dehydrated. You don't notice the time passing, your mind's not on your work. You spend an inordinate amount of money and feel no responsibility. Your thunderstruck mind is bewitched by never-ending experiences of searing intensity. Your life is teeming with plans and ideas. You laugh a lot.

Psychiatry would see in this all the signs of an attack of mania, a pathology with a clinical description that faithfully reproduces all the symptoms of electrocution by lightning: hydro-electrolytic disturbances, massive dehydration. Treatment is needed. The victim of light-ning is resuscitated, he is made to drink, his burnt skin is bandaged, his body is wrapped.

In what were once called 'manic-depressive' and are now called 'bipolar' disorders, we know that the eupho-ria of the attack of mania gives way to depression. Just as suddenly as the Mania comes on, It disappears and you plunge into the abyss. What is It? The god of mania, a sacred madness we can no longer see.

The lovers' *coup de foudre* doesn't turn into its oppo-site as suddenly as the attack of mania. Because the *coup de foudre* has, in the West where it appeared, a certain exalted status, it's granted some time socially. The plunge into the abyss comes much later.

When lovers emerge from their eclipse, their world is no longer the same. They start work again, they get back into life. Generally, that life has to be repaired and almost everything has to be changed. They have to attend to the wreckage and start earning money again. Resuscitating, bandaging, wrapping. They're into a new life but it's a life all the same. Life is tiring, it is humdrum. And time is back, you're not in the eclipse any more. Most often you get used to it. Not always. It isn't so easy to reconstruct a world you've wrecked.

And this world has been wrecked since the twelfth century when the *coup de foudre* was publicly recognized.

It's as though suddenly, throughout the whole of Christian Europe, the first romances lent enchantment to adultery. It's an epidemic running through the aristocracy, a new, heroic *mal d'amour*, an indestructible heterosexual model. The court poets sing the praises of two adulterous couples who refuse to put off their lovers' crowns, who won't give in or repent. Uncontrollable.

Those living in the eclipse of life are always uncontrollable.

On a sea voyage, Tristan, a king's nephew, and Princess Iseult partake of the same goblet of wine. Iseult is the distant, foreign fiancée whom Tristan has conquered for another—for his uncle. He owes her respect; she is off-limits to him. But they each have a past and the wine is 'herbed'—poisoned with love—for Iseult is a sorceress in Ireland, her country of origin.

She has tended to the wounded Tristan, though she hated him for killing her husband in combat, hated him and watched him as he rested. With the purulence of his wounds gone, Iseult came to find her husband's killer handsome. She allowed herself to be led like a cow to the bull, not understanding that the bull wouldn't be Tristan but a king, an old king she has never seen.

At the moment of the *coup de foudre*, the fair Iseult was still the prize Tristan was taking home to his uncle

King Mark. But with the first gulp of wine her emotions are in turmoil. 'If you had not been there,' she tells him in the Carlisle version, 'I would have known nothing of love . . . the sea . . . bitterness.' Her words are muddled or won't come at all. 'Seasickness, nausea?' asks Tristan. 'No,' replies Iseult, 'it's my heart that's oppressed and I'm suffocating. This *amour/amertume* (love/bitterness) comes from the *mer/amour* (sea/love) and it began as soon as we embarked.'

For all her invention, Tristan will soon disentangle *l'amer*, *l'amour* and *la mer* (bitterness, love and the sea): 'Yes, yes. My pain has the same origin as yours. It's not from *la mer* that it comes, but from *l'amour*, and it was at sea (*en mer*) that love seized hold of me.' What great clarity! Then, says the text, 'They open their hearts to each other and kiss, they embrace each other and give themselves over to pleasure.' No longer is there just a moment—there is all eternity. But the rest of the time Iseult remains the betrothed of Tristan's uncle. His future aunt.

It's all this that's eclipsed—marriage, kinship and 'the rest of the time'.

The incestuous *coup de foudre* eclipses adultery. In this same period in the Vulgate Cycle of the Grail romance, the handsome Sir Lancelot appears, with fiery eyes, chestnut-golden hair and dimpled chin. He has killed many and captured many. He is a young knight raised in a lake. King Arthur and his queen welcome him and Lancelot sits himself down on the green grass strewn about the great hall. He takes a surreptitious glance at the queen, no longer able to restrain himself. She is the forbidden woman.

The queen takes his hand and he starts, 'as though awaking suddenly'. Lancelot has fallen into deep contemplation of Queen Guinevere and is to remain in that state.

She has no such reaction. Guinevere pretends to think him rather simple-minded. Too young! Still a child. Though Lancelot is sent into raptures when she takes his hand—'bare flesh against bare flesh'—she seems indifferent. But the lightning is making its way, bare flesh against bare flesh . . . The height of the eclipse is their lying naked side by side, motionless, through the night. Skin against skin, the first feeding of the beast-with-two-backs.

This is a chaste meeting. They mingle their saliva but the sperm stays in its—warm—place. Before Lancelot may penetrate Guinevere, he must spend many moons adventuring—saving damsels by the score, slaying monsters, defeating knights and also disappearing, passing incognito.

From repeatedly asking, 'Who is this stranger?' Guinevere will end up deceiving King Arthur as Iseult deceived King Mark.

A *coup de foudre* in the very moment, and that moment will last until the point when Iseult, now King Mark's wife, is a queen under surveillance. She risks being burnt at the stake, but what of it? She leaves her husband, he abandons his uncle. And, leaving society behind, they head off into the forest with the animals.

Young Lancelot falls in love with Queen Guinevere, who will bring him all manner of suffering. To help her, he climbs into the cart of the condemned (*la charrette des malfrats*) like a common criminal. But because he hesitated for the time it takes to take two steps before clambering into it, she treats him with cold cruelty. Two steps! He braves her coldness.

Moses was similarly punished by the God of the Bible for striking the rock twice rather than once to make the waters flow. Insufficient trust—Moses will not enter the Promised Land, he will die just before reaching it.

These love-crazed couples inflict suffering on each other with a very precise aim—to reach the point of fusion they call Joy. This doesn't come spontaneously, they have first to be tested. They have first to fall, then to be reborn, to change their lives. But when Joy arrives, then they are outside their bodies, outside life. The lovers are eclipsed to the point where you'd think they were no longer visible.

They're irresistible. None can stand in their way. Neither kings nor their entourages, neither priests nor God. No one. They've chosen eclipse and they'll hold to it. They'll suffer hunger and cold and live as vagabonds, survive on husks and live as savages but, against all expectations, they'll not be punished. Quite the reverse. Wreathed in a Joy that puts such harsh pressures on them, they'll be honoured down the centuries.

Old-fashioned notions? We may think so; almost a thousand years have passed. What can we make of this?

The adulterous *coup de foudre* comes at a strange moment in the Middle Ages. After the Crusades, with the nobles encountering demands from clerics, the poor gentry and even the peasantry, the chivalric romances defend heroes who defy the wider community—pure individualists with wild dreams of escaping from the social body. Their love is wild. Is this because it is forbidden? Not entirely.

In accordance with the rules of courtly love, and however misleading these may be about the supposed power of the 'ladies' of the courts, the—lordly—husbands show kindness. As professional armies loom on the horizon, solid battalions of soldiers properly recruited and trained, the old knightly order is in terminal decline. Deprived of heroism, it tolerates these *vacances amoureuses* which produce no children and lead nowhere. Love is impossible. Proof is provided by the *coup de foudre*. Sublime but unreal.

No return to reality. No procreation. The noble husband allows matters to take their course. And the only progeny is death.

Arabia, five centuries earlier. Qays, whose sight is poor, falls in love with his cousin Layla when they are both still children. But, in contravention of the tribe's code of honour, the rash young man proclaims his love out loud. To reassert his authority, the tribal chief marries off Layla to another and Qays goes mad—*majnun*. He becomes a moonstruck vagabond. When Layla, flanked by chaperones, turns up at his door, Qays refuses to see her, since he loves her so madly the real Layla would detract from his love. From this point on, he calls himself Majnun-Layla. He no longer has need of her. He goes off into the desert, living with the animals, so possessed with love that he'll die there an ascetic, dressed in mystic rags, raving over the Layla he believes he sees in the tiniest pebble. Reduced to its bare bones, the Majnun's love succeeds in disposing of the need for the actual woman.

This old patriarchal model, reproduced indefinitely, is inexhaustibly simple—a young boy loves another man's wife with an impossible love that turns him into either hero or madman. Or, in the bourgeois version—and once the amorous crisis has passed—into a manly adult. What remains of the amorous eclipse that stuns, liberates and affords such joy?

In France, adultery hasn't been punished by law since 1975; a wife is no longer precisely 'another man's woman' and marriage isn't much of a commitment. It's no longer an offence to fall in love with a married woman, nor a heroic act. It's barely an adventure or, even less, a cause for excitement. It's something banal. People fall in and out of love. Seldom do we meet with old-style *coups de foudre*.

Yet they are still to be seen, as in the following famous instance. According to legend, Nicolas Sarkozy, a married man and a father, fell in love with a woman whom, in his functions as mayor of Neuilly and as official registrar for that suburb, he was marrying to another man. And he did so at that precise moment.

He took years to win her hand, but eventually did so and was married to her before the appropriate authorities. The sequel to this adventure—the fact that his wife would later leave him very publicly and he would divorce (for a second time) then marry a sort of fairy—in no way compromises the *coup-de-foudre* moment of Nicolas-Lancelot and Cécilia-Guinevere.

More seriously, crimes of love, sometimes termed 'crimes of passion', occur frequently in many countries, including France. When a furiously jealous man is involved and holes himself up with a weapon, the authorities tend to speak of a 'dangerous maniac', someone 'ferocious, violent, fearsome, excessive, hysterical and out of control'. This always prompts the intervention of specialized police units. The dangerous maniac's discharging of his firearm usually leaves three or four people dead.

At the other end of the world, in the village-based societies where the patriarchy violently defends its rights over the opposite sex, a father, a brother, a cousin or other male family members slaughter rebellious girls or women with impunity. They have authority to do so. They call this 'honour'. A girl is an item of property like a plot of land or a calf.

In the *Universal Declaration of Human Rights*, Article 16(2) states that 'Marriage shall be entered into only with the free and full consent of the intending spouses.'

This is one of the battlefields that divides the world between those who permit love matches and those who forbid them. Ninety-nine per cent of Indian marriages are arranged by families. At stake here is the freedom of girls.

Layla today would suffer an acid attack.

This is true in Turkey and true in Pakistan. It is true, alas, in India, where it is a new phenomenon, notably in the state of Haryana where, out in the villages, Hindu parents murder modern young lovers who aren't from the same caste and have stopped obeying their elders. The girl is buried alive.

Over there, the *coup de foudre* is still awaiting official acceptance but you can feel it coming like a freshly brewing storm. You can glimpse it in Bollywood films; you can see the storm clouds gathering, ready to discharge their lightning.

How is it that this old refrain keeps coming back? There's a literature on it in Europe; it's kept alive in fiction, in films and TV series, tragic or satirical. Guinevere becomes 'the little woman', Lancelot a haughty, posh boy and Perceval an idiot, while King Arthur resembles a small town mayor, but the story still has legs.

It speaks of the *coup de foudre* and the ravages it produces, of the post-*coup-de-foudre* state, the ruses of a new life, how that life falls apart and how you weary of it, how you want so greatly to recover the Joy that you prefer to die—it is simpler.

Tristan will experience madness. Lancelot too. They will be humiliated, scorned. They will live in the dirt. Tristan and Lancelot will be caught with traces of blood spurting from their lovers' wounds when, with prodigious leaps, they spring from their own beds to their lovers' in chambers where they do not sleep alone. This will, of course, be the death of them. Though never at the same time. And they don't confess their misdeeds. Even though Lancelot knows his love will deprive him of the Grail, he refuses to abjure 'the sweetest and finest sin' he has ever committed, and Tristan prefers death to the wife he has married in order to dispel the image of Iseult.

The women, for their part, put up with the situation. They will be confronted with their imperfect doubles. Tristan marries an Iseult with white hands who is an Iseult in name alone. And King Arthur is tricked by a fake Guinevere whom he loves more than the real one. The neglected queens fall into sadness, get themselves to nunneries, cut off their long hair. They don't eat much, they weep and they grow ugly. Iseult will revive only on the point of death, and Queen Guinevere, taken back by her repentant husband, will eventually die alone, far from Lancelot.

Far-off stories. But be that as it may. The lovers are buried side by side; a rose tree and a vine spring up from their graves and intertwine, dumbfounding all onlookers. This miracle of the plant kingdom has a meaning. It was permissible then, after all?

Yes, after all. Woe to those who've never known the marvellous trance that nothing can resist. Such people are to be pitied. Yet they are legion. They are the normal ones. You have to be crazy to experience the *coup de foudre*. This is what those around these sudden lovers never tire of repeating: 'Come to your senses, now!'

What the tales of the chivalric age tell us is that the lover's trance is a blessing. Amid the single combat, the battles and the derring-do, the only hymn that rises above the forest trees is a hymn to love, and that love is adulterous. Guilty and permitted.

But it has a double.

CHAPTER 2

Three Drops of Blood

The 'Matter of Brittany' comprises the Breton legends of the twelfth and thirteenth centuries. In these Arthurian romances, there aren't many who have seen the Grail. At most, three or four knights.

In the vessel on which Jesus shared his last supper with his disciples, Joseph of Arimathea gathered Christ's blood after the Crucifixion. This platter, goblet or bowl resides in the castle of the Fisher King, a cripple. The Fisher King offers a splendid welcome to passing knights and, without warning, as they lie on the banqueting couch, he inflicts an ordeal on each of them.

In a brilliantly lit hall, there pass before the guests a squire holding a lance of whitest iron with a drop of blood on its tip, damsels carrying two large candlesticks with flaming candles in them and a golden platter so pure and radiant that the candles pale beside it. The lance, the candlesticks and the platter pass round once, twice, then once again before exiting. That is all.

The first knight, Perceval, feared above all to go against the advice he had received—to hold his tongue and not say too much. So, when he saw the mysterious procession, Perceval said nothing. He would like to have known but he didn't dare ask. The imperative, above all, was not to talk. The banquet continued and off he went to bed. When he awoke, there was no one there. No trace of a feast. Perceval was alone.

A maiden he meets in a wood bemoans his actions and explains his mistake. The Fisher King was expecting questions! These questions, which should have been asked, would have restored the unhappy king and saved the world!

The second knight, Gawain, King Arthur's nephew, stares so fixedly at the Grail that he believes he sees a candle burning inside it, so brightly does the object shine. And when the lance passes, he seems to see two angels carrying lighted golden candlesticks. Bedazzled, he is lost in thought, 'seized by a joy so intense that he forgets everything and thinks only of God'. When the Grail passes again, he believes he sees three angels; when it's the turn of the lance, he sees a child. At that very moment, three drops of blood fall on to the white tablecloth.

Gawain holds out his hand but the drops of blood slip through and he experiences an infinite sadness. A third time the Grail passes by with its damsels. Gawain raises his eyes and sees a man on the cross with a lance in his side. And he remains like this, looking upwards. The damsels and the squire disappear. The table is cleared. Sir Gawain is alone.

He has asked no questions.

The third knight, Lancelot, is much more talkative and converses happily with the Fisher King. He brings news and receives a message which he promises to pass on. Everything goes swimmingly. But no damsel comes carrying the Grail, no squire bearing a lance. Guilty of an unrepentant love of Queen Guinevere, Lancelot is a man obsessed. She occupies all his thoughts and there's no place for the Grail.

Gawain and Lancelot each have their eclipse—mystical in the former case, erotic in the latter. If they don't ask questions, it's because they're otherwise occupied. Lost in *panser*—lost in thought.

Thinking is a trance. When it comes to saving the world, eclipses have no place in it.

But Perceval? If he doesn't ask questions, it's from fear of doing the wrong thing. Perceval is the innocent idiot, the 'young savage' whom his dear mother has protected from the world without telling him either his own name or his father's. Altered states, Perceval?—come off it! They think him beyond redemption . . . but they're wrong.

After choking back his questions at the Grail castle, Perceval passes a flight of cackling wild geese dazzled by the snow and fleeing a falcon. A wounded goose escapes and, as it flies off, three drops of blood bespatter the snow. Perceval pulls up short.

Blood and snow, red and white like the cheeks of his friend Blancheflor whom he loves so much and has just left. Oh that chaste night, mouth to mouth stark naked in the same bed!

Leaning on his lance, Perceval forgets who and where he is. His consciousness is eclipsed by three drops of blood spilt by a goose wounded by a falcon.

They come out to look for him but he doesn't reply. They believe he has fallen asleep, call out to him, reprimand him. He responds furiously, killing the king's brother. Then, with that annoyance out of the way, he leans back on his lance and falls into contemplation once more. He'll snap out of it only when the snow melts and the drops of blood left by the wild goose eclipse themselves.

Returning to his senses, he tells how 'Two people came who wanted to steal my Joy from me and take me away . . .' And he, the wild one, didn't want to leave the three drops of blood on the white of the snow, the portrait of his lady-friend.

Gawain thinks him right in this. His was a licensed eclipse. 'You'd have to be mad or quite brutal to wish to have anyone fall out of love with her,' says the text.

Three drops of blood are enough to trigger a trance. Three red drops against white—of tablecloth or snow. The object? It's a part-object. Blancheflor's cheek, luminous angels, the outline of a man on a cross—diffuse evocations. Three drops of blood forming on the side of a wild duck or at the tip of an enigmatic lance—is that enough to deflect the necessary questions? Yes. Rather than ask the questions, eclipse oneself. You'll have plenty of time to grow up later.

Not now.

In a masterful piece of writing, Lévi-Strauss explains that Perceval is the opposite of Oedipus. Oedipus answers the Sphinx's questions while Perceval fails to ask the questions about the Grail. The former joins the answer to his question—too much communication—while the latter avoids joining the two—lack of communication. Question and answer are an accursed pair, like the parental couple. The question can be seen as the mother and the answer the son. The incestuous Oedipus will join the two together, a tragic success. As for Perceval, who has remained chaste, he is far removed from incest and as infertile as the *gaste terre*—the sterile land—of an infirm king wounded in the thigh. Oedipus replies from too close up, Perceval leaves the question too far off.

A last knight sees the Grail. This is Galahad. He is pure. He doesn't ask questions, since he knows it all already. He knows that the Grail, a chalice, contains the blood of Jesus Christ; that the lance is the one which pierced his side; and that all that's needed to heal the maimed king is to touch him and life will return. Galahad the pure takes the lance, touches the groin of the Fisher King who then rises up and walks. Galahad will die celebrating the cult and all is completed. There's so little mystery that in a stroke of genius, in their play *Graal Théâtre*, Florence Delay and Jacques Roubaud transformed Galahad into an actual robot.

No risk of eclipse. Galahad for president.

But three drops of blood are better, aren't they?

CHAPTER 3

Filth

The trance has its underside and that's filth. Lovers experience it, as do mad knights. In the theatre of trance, the stage has wings where the performance is all about dirt. It's in the wings, in a room off limits to everyone, that they give the raw meat to the lion-cook. It's there that they daub the bodies with blood and faeces. In Central Africa, 'filth'—*la saleté*—is the name of the magical object that attacks and destroys.

Let's take the women in the trance at Dakar. To enter the dance, they all followed the same path.

First, the attack—languor, shivering, anorexia, headaches, paralysed bodies and dreams beckoning the unknown spirit whose property they are without realizing it.

Second, consultation—the trance-master or mistress strives to discover the name of the proprietary spirit by divination: a gourd filled with water and bits of floating wood, a sieve covered with millet and a twig stuck in it.

Third, the ritual—the butcher cuts the throat of the sacrificial animal and the women recover the blood, still warm, in a number of gourds. Some is drunk by the mistress of the rite. The rest will have its uses. Not a drop must be spilt. One day, when the first gourd had been set down askew, the animal's blood ran off and reddened the sand. Great lamentations! Where was the missing blood to be found?

Depending on available finances, the animals will be cockerels, rams and, invariably, a bull. The mistress of the rite will, with all her might, aim a carefully thrown raw egg against the bull's side. The egg breaks and trickles down. Just as the dying beast shudders, its last breath and its blood flow from it with the whites of the eggs.

Fourth, treatment—bandaged and concealed in white sheets, the long-suffering women free themselves only to be daubed from head to foot in blood. Women covered with viscous substances, like the newborn that has just left its mother's vulva, the building of the altar of the spirit that is within them. They belong to it and they do so for life.

Finally, on the last day, washed, changed, transformed and wearing fresh clothes, they'll perhaps be able to enter the sand circle for their first trance, celebrating the spirit for which their body provides a temple.

Among the Bamana who live in Mali, *boli* are immensely sacred figures, vaguely resembling cattle in shape. Their outer skin of dried clay conceals a wooden carcase stuffed with secret substances, chewed nuts, millet, bark, animal blood and human sperm. And, of course, excrement.

We find this everywhere. For the yogis of India, the most sacred drink is not pure water but a liquid composed of five elements from the cow: milk, whey, cream, urine and dung. Dung! Peasant women plaster it on the walls of their houses, imprinting the mark of their spread fingers on it, producing something like a ravishing flower of shit. And the beaten-earth floor is disinfected with urine.

In *The Horse Boy*, the author Rupert Isaacson, a Briton with an American wife, has an autistic son who has no control of his anal sphincters. He's a boy of twelve who screams almost all the time, except around horses which nuzzle up to him in a kindly way. After studying the trances of the Bushman therapists of the Kalahari desert, his father has the idea of taking him to see a number of shamans in Mongolia, the land where the horse first appeared. It's a crazy idea but it works.

First, before doing anything else, the shamans vigorously whip the parents. Then, the child. Finally, they go into a trance. At the end of a treatment, one of the Mongol shamans gives the autistic child some therapeutic nourishment—a reindeer's belly stuffed with reindeer dung. He knows nothing of this.

The child will no longer spread his shit just anywhere.

In Siberia, the newly initiated shaman will carefully gather up the dung of the deer whose skin he wears to perform his functions. And, because I, myself, when I was a child, participated in the village pig ceremony, I know that in the *andouille*—white pudding—even when it's carefully cleaned, a little shit remains. 'That's what gives it the taste,' they used to say.

Work on dirty material demands clear-sightedness. You don't go eclipsing yourself in the kitchens of the gods. It's a serious occupation that requires time and meticulousness. It needs great attention and calmness. You're barely even allowed to sing. You're away from prying eyes. The drums are silent. At Dakar, I thought I saw the women who were dancing last night doing embroidery. What are they doing? And with what?

With the guts of the bull, the trance-mistress and her aides are making garlands sown into red cotton— these wrapped innards act as charms. The impure offal will be protective. Morarji Desai, a prime minister of India, who died on the evening of his hundredth birthday, prided himself on drinking his own urine each morning. 'Urine therapy' he called it on national television, evoking Mithridates.

In the same way, during lovemaking, we see the mingling of substances, none of them impure, in the 'beast with two backs'. There's drinking, sucking, licking, swallowing. Having watched a Bamana *boli* being made, the anthropologist Jean Bazin quoted Wittgenstein, 'Man is a ceremonial animal. He manufactures the sacred with real materials.'

But the Grail contains blood that doesn't coagulate. And you wouldn't break an egg—which might germinate—against the Grail.

Red matter drips from the lance and melts into the snow. It's the blood of the wild goose or perhaps even the blood of Christ, but it doesn't dry. It will never be possible to make a fetish out of it.

CHAPTER 4

Rutting Reindeer

Figures from 2010 suggest that fifteen million French people visited clairvoyants in that year.

This is the—now pale—reflection of a universal practice which, to help keep itself in being, has need of the trance. Popularized by films in which special effects perform their wonders, shamanism now forms part of the Western imaginary landscape. We see an entranced Patrick Bruel sporting vertically slit jaguar's eyes or Catherine Deneuve transformed into a murderous she-bear. In literary and cinematic fiction, humans endowed with supernatural powers become thinking animals that kill.

The origins of real shamanism are in Siberia among the Buryat, Tungus, Yakut, Evenk and Mongol peoples. In *La Chasse à l'âme*, a positive breviary of Siberian shamanism, the anthropologist Roberte Hamayon describes the making of shamans and the furious trance that gives them second sight.

It's an infinitely cautious process. An infant will not be allowed to come into contact with the 'super nature' within which the shamans move. If he cries abnormally, if the presence of a spirit is suspected, efforts will be made to drive it away. It's too early and too dangerous.

It's at puberty that the signs are acknowledged which, when listed, resemble, with the exception of one element, the symptoms of spirit-possession among the women of the Dakar region. Anorexia, languidness, sleepiness, delirium, fainting, dreams—the whole catalogue.

The different Siberian element is flight into the forest. Disappearance into the shade of the larches.

In all worlds, to run distraught from one's house—to leave home, to rove and wander—indicates the call of the trance. For the Dogon people, it's in such sudden flight that the screaming 'totemic priest' runs off in search of his sacred stone. When he finds it and hangs it round his neck on the end of a strip of leather, the trance ends and with it the shouting.

Anger and rebellion produce this effect. Leaving, quitting, breaking off . . .

Slipping far away from human beings, eclipsing oneself—a Siberian shaman's first absconding indicates absence of the soul. It may be spontaneous or simulated—the question matters little insofar as the structuring of a shaman is concerned. It's a crisis state, the mark of a chosenness which, if all goes well, will become a choice of career. Families fear these absences among their young, even if they've encouraged their occurrence and even if it appears that the adolescent is deliberately simulating in order to become a shaman. For being chosen as a shaman is not without its dangers—the future shaman will become the husband of a female spirit, the daughter of the forest.

If he refuses this marriage or ends it, he may die as a consequence. Such things have been seen.

The group, in fear and trembling, gives up one of its members to a supernatural bride who brooks no evasion.

The apprentice shaman will have to be a tireless lover to his spirit wife; otherwise, she will take another. The daughter of the forest has demanding auxiliaries—they wish to eat the flesh of the chosen one, to drink his blood. This is why, during the crisis, the young shaman grows thinner—this state of being devoured ends when the ritual that confirms his status ends. Before that, his body is open to the spirits which feed on it, and in this untamed state the young boy is defenceless. Loving and lean.

As in the *coup de foudre*, eclipsing oneself from life causes one to grow thin. In each case there's a devouring. A necessary change of body and hence of flesh.

But after the ritual, once the shaman is made, the spirits find doors closed to them. They now have only two entrances: his mouth—this is why the shaman yawns such a lot at the beginning of the séance—and/or his armpits—this is why his costume is not stitched up beneath the arms.

And girls? They too shamanize. Not when they are pregnant or menstruating. But the rest of the time female shamans are said to be more dangerous than the male, since they can use their menstrual blood to combat males. It's of no avail for male shamans to feminize their costumes. They're no rivals for the power of menstrual blood, universally conceived as a threat.

Having mentioned their costume, let's take a close look at it.

The basic garment is the pelt of a cervid—a reindeer or an elk. On that pelt the Siberian shaman wears, stitched into the back, nine complete 'snouts' (sable, squirrel, stoat, marten, polecat, otter, fox, hare and roe deer), metal pendants, a miniaturized knife and axe, little bells, spirals of cones, animal and human figurines strung together, ribbons and patches of fabric.

His head sports an iron crown made of two interlocking semicircles and surmounted by iron antlers or sometimes a sabre. Eagle feathers may be added.

On his feet the shaman wears boots made from the skin of a cervid and decorated with pieces of its hooves. Two rules go with this costume, called 'armour': in exercizing his functions, a shaman must not go barefoot or bare-headed.

And, indeed, you might mistake him for a knight from the Grail stories, clad in armour, protected by a shield sporting an animal figure—a dancing leopard or a lion with a raised paw.

The costume is complemented by the so-called horse-sticks. The head of a horse is carved at the top of these; lower down there is a knee and, at the bottom, a hoof. If the costume is the shaman's armour, the stick is his mount. He works with a 'drum'—which may be an instrument of taut animal skin with a deer or elk drawn on it—or a bell, a rope or even a frying pan. And, in order to speak the language of the spirits, the shaman needs a Jew's harp or a hurdy-gurdy.

A deer skin, deer boots, a drawing of a deer on the skin drum whose sound reproduces 'belling' or 'troating' . . .

Shamans make no secret of the fact that they are like rutting reindeer. Their human identity is complemented by another animal identity. If they have several alliances in the spirit world, they will also be eagles, bears and bulls. When they speak to their wives, who are daughters of the forest, they call them with an animal cry, in a voice very different from the one they use to relate their adventure to humans. And the apprentice's rituals begin with the skin of the cervid that the human must wear in order to take over all of its behaviour—running the way it does, belling or troating the way it does.

The 'animation' of the drum, a series of complex acts which confer its soul on the instrument, includes a phase in which the shaman seeks out the place where the reindeer which gave him its skin was born, collecting *in situ* the hair, bones and even excrement of the men and animals who've eaten its flesh.

He's now ready.

In the séance, the shaman jumps, leaps, trembles and shudders. He's in the state of an excited reindeer seeking his female. His cries are a belling. He has changed body. Then, as the norm dictates, he falls down as if dead. He isn't breathing and has no pulse.

The two moments are necessary—erotic fury for the animal rutting; inertia to return, thereafter, to the human state.

Are they mad? No. After the séance, the shamans behave entirely normally. Can we say they're cured of a genuine madness channelled by their shamanistic activity? Perhaps we can.

According to Hamayon, however, shamanizing also enables heroic popular personalities to emerge. In undergoing trances, these 'heroic popular personalities' no doubt pass through a form of deviance essential to popularity. Those who whip up crowds need this intoxication. Look at them at rallies—they're beside themselves. Returning from these states is difficult. The deviance may linger.

Are they drugged? They certainly fast, a practice which encourages hallucinations. They smoke and, in some cases, consume hallucinogenic mushrooms. Or strong liquor. Going into trance states for one's group is a risky business. Suddenly, I'm put in mind of the soldiers of the Great War who were given a 'snifter' by their officers to get them out of the trenches and 'over the top'. That snifter was a rough brandy that made you capable of killing.

The nagging question of simulation presents itself. In Siberia it doesn't matter. To simulate a flight into the woods is to flee into the woods. But what of the others? Are the trance-queens of the Dakar region simulating? Many Westerners ask themselves the question. Africans rarely do. The Westerner needs scientific proof; he's almost prepared to go and fiddle with their eyelids to check that their eyes really are rolling. Where possible, he provides an explanation: you just have to press firmly on the neck, there at the top, and you fall into a trance. It's as easy as that. He doesn't accept the in-between state of the crisis, the beautiful uncertainty of the troubled consciousness. He wants something solid—genuine convulsions. He doesn't want to be caught out.

But the trance catches you.

Since we're talking about an eminently public scene, the simulation of the trance state is like Diderot's paradox of the comedian. Is he sensate, capable of receiving impressions and experiencing emotions, or is he, rather, coldly lucid? Sincere or a fraud? In fact he's both. This is what Alfred Métraux describes in *Voodoo in Haiti* (1972). Inflamed by the desire to be mounted by his divinity, an initiate wants to go into a trance. He gets into position, begins to simulate and his *loa* responds to his call; another, by contrast, will try in vain to escape that state. It's a question, he tells us, that 'drops out'.

Leiris termed *théâtre vécu* (lived theatre) the séances during which his healer friend served as a coat rack for many spirits. In 2002, studying the trances induced by the *tromba* spirits on the island of Mayotte, the anthropologist Bertrand Hell set to work with specialists on hypnosis and found that, in this very closely trance-related phenomenon, 'loss of control' expresses itself in changes in the anterior cingulate cortex, the brainstem and the thalamus, changes made visible through neuro-imaging techniques. Whether induced by simulation or spontaneous, whether one identity is being added to another or actually taking over, the change, we may conclude, is a reality. But it cannot be dissociated from the social context or from the procedures surrounding shamanism.

The shaman is an illusionist. Lévi-Strauss explains this with great clarity when he analyses the famous memoirs of Quesalid, alias George Hunt, an Amerindian of mixed race (with a Scottish father and a Tlingit mother), who was raised in the Kwakiutl world and taught the kwakwaka'wakw language by the great American anthropologist Franz Boas. Quesalid didn't believe in the powers of the sorcerers, employed subterfuge to have himself initiated, uncovered the tricks involved in their healing techniques, but then went on to apply these rigorously, convinced of their efficacy.

In Quesalid's world, the subterfuges the shamans learnt were conjuring tricks using rattles and head-rings; a biting technique that enabled the shaman to make his gums bleed and redden a hidden tuft of down which he then spat out, spitting out 'the illness itself'; and the employment of 'dreamers', spies discreetly tasked with listening to gossip and family secrets.

Now, Quesalid gradually became persuaded that these particular acts of fakery were better than others. And he did in fact cure his patients, because he wasn't the owner of the illusion. He shared it with the social body. Sceptical and determined, Quesalid would in fact be sincere without even trying.

In Siberia, an adolescent who dreams of being a shaman may simulate the signs of the soul's escape, may run off alone into the forest deliberately, without first being inspired to do so, and have a good, lifelong career as a shaman. On the circle of sand, a woman may simulate possession by her snake-spirit and crawl with her hands grasped behind her and her back out of joint. She may throw her head violently to and fro and bring herself down amid the drums; nonetheless she goes down in one fell swoop. Is she doing this coldly, like the good actor, or is she in fact extremely sensitive? The social body is indifferent about this. Simulating doesn't prevent you from taking a holiday from life, and the body exiting from life will be no less happy for it.

The lion-woman would have liked to have been simulating.

Hamayon terms the shaman's transient madness 'erotic fury', since this wildness shows the sexual union with the spirit wife, the supernatural girl. An assistant is present to prevent him from falling, since this lover's fury has to let itself rip. There is jumping and leaping, spasmodic shaking, cries and convulsions. Once this first moment is past, the shaman must fall. But not just anywhere. On a ritual carpet, as this second moment is the moment of death, a death from which he must return. The space for the return is therefore carefully delimited. If the shaman is slow to rise again, the assistant will make sparks fly to bring him back into the human world.

And the last moment is the moment of storytelling—in a voice that is once again human, the shaman tells of his journey, his meetings with spirits, his warlike adventures, events into which his fury disappears. This is the time of vision.

Sometimes, the wildness spills over into life. There's no transforming yourself into a rutting reindeer with impunity. The inner beast seethes with impatience. It demands its belling, its antler fights, its juddering rear.

What's to be done with the shaman who turns savage in everyday life? They should have been wary of him, as he wasn't entirely stable. He ceases at this point to be a shaman and is simply regarded as mad.

We find these erotic animal frenzies elsewhere. The Majnun in the desert lives with the gazelles and, like them, eats grass. In the Grail Cycle, Chrétien de Troyes tells the story of a knight who experiences this same madness.

Yvain, married to Laudine who would like to keep him in the conjugal cocoon, wants to go adventuring with the knights of Arthur's court. Before he leaves, Laudine, a fearsome figure, sets a deadline for her loving husband. He must return in one year's time or she'll render her husband 'haggard and downcast'. Under the threat of this curse Yvain leaves or, rather, his body leaves, for his heart stays with the woman he loves. Or so the story says.

This remains to be seen. Yvain goes from tourney to tourney, has a splendid time and lets the deadline pass. Laudine rejects him as she had sworn to. As a result, Yvain goes mad.

His madness begins when he's overcome by a bout of dizziness. He tears his clothing, steals a bow and arrows from a little boy and goes off into the woods where he lives stark naked. Starving, he wolfs down mouldy bread given to him by a hermit who also leaves a dead beast outside his door each day. Is he an animal?

With the slaughtered hinds and stags the good hermit cooks venison. Yvain doesn't eat raw meat. There is, however, a sign that Yvain has been a stag. When he returns to his senses, feeling shame at his nudity, he no longer knows how to walk on two feet. He has no doubt been hunting on all fours.

To reacquire human status, he has need of a salve created by a fairy. But the animal within him hasn't disappeared. He meets a lion who dogs his steps, defends him when he's attacked, sleeps with him and licks his hands, which leads Chrétien de Troyes to name him 'the knight with the lion'. Because he has passed through madness and tapped into the animal world, Yvain is a shaman.

This is what the trance does—it taps into animality.

In the Arthurian cycle, there's no disquiet and no suspicion. Discreet as they are, still and silent, the knights' trances are highly respectable; to disturb them is a sin. Whatever its cause—a woman's gaze or drops of blood—the trance is a moment of sacred inspiration.

Four centuries later, after the Black Plague, the age of discovery, the expulsion of the Jews—and, later, of the Moors—and once the wars of religion have calmed down again in Europe, the trance becomes a thing of witchcraft.

CHAPTER 5

Cats on the Ends of Branches (Poitou-Charentes)

Lying in the Vienne department in the Poitou-Charentes region of France, Loudun, a 'town in bloom', with its esplanades and Festival of Young Talent at the Sainte-Croix collegiate church, has at the dawn of the twenty-first century eight thousand, eleven hundred and eleven residents.

Loudun, a fortified town and a solid Protestant fortress which the Catholic powers have designs on, has in the middle of the seventeenth century fourteen thousand inhabitants.

In 1632, plague suddenly breaks out, killing more than three thousand between May and September.

To protect themselves, before fleeing to the country, the members of the medical profession recommend that people carry perfumed materials about their person. For the rich, aloe, terebinth and, above all, roses; for the poor, laurel, rosemary and cypress, to be burnt in the home. Flight and perfume are the only remedies. Some decamp at speed, others turn to fragrant smells. Loudun is in turmoil.

The plague epidemic is coming to an end when another epidemic breaks out in late September. Erotic frenzies in a convent.

The heroine of this fabulous saga, which set the whole area alight, is a reverend mother of some thirty years of age, the prioress of the convent of Ursuline nuns at Loudun.

Mother Jeanne des Anges, the daughter of noble Gascon parents, was born into a family of fifteen children, her mother having experienced nineteen pregnancies. As a young girl, she had a fall. The precise circumstances aren't known. The accident dislocated her shoulder and her body remained crooked, one shoulder distinctly higher than the other.

Her mother, Mme de Crozes, immediately decided that the deformed girl would be sent to a nunnery. When she introduced her other daughters into society, she dressed them well, but not Jeanne. A suitor was turned away and Jeanne entered the Ursuline convent of Poitiers in 1622.

By her own admission she was not a good nun. She made a great show of her devotion, was most unruly and, on one occasion, spectacularly announced her intention to leave in front of the whole convent. In 1625, a new Ursuline nunnery was created at Loudun and Sister Jeanne des Anges employed all manner of subterfuge to get round her Mother Superior and assume its leadership. She succeeded in this thanks to what she describes as her 'thousand little adaptabilities of mind'. So there she was at Loudun, prioress of the Convent of the Daughters of Saint Ursula.

A gifted but misshapen schemer. A gracious, pretty young woman with ash-blond hair.

Things started at the convent with apparitions at the end of September—apparitions of a father confessor who had died some weeks before, and of a man seen from behind, a violent, dark ball of a man. In early October, the dark shadow acquired a name—Urbain Grandier, parish priest of the church of Saint-Pierre du Marché at Loudun.

Two years later, this proud, worthy hero would be condemned to death for sorcery. Burnt alive. Though the cases of possession would simply go on increasing in number.

The presumed sorcerer did his work with flowers. On the first day of October, a hand placed three hawthorn branches in the palm of the prioress and closed her fingers over them. The first convulsions occurred the next day. Ten days later, Mother Jeanne des Anges found a bunch of three musk roses on the dormitory steps, red roses with a musky scent.

Before it was produced synthetically with the aim of protecting biodiversity, musk came from a little gland of the rutting musk deer, an animal that lives in Siberia. The male odour the sorcerer gives off is a musky smell.

Who had put the roses there? Jeanne picked them up, raised them to her nose and handed them to her companions who also sniffed them. The effect was instantaneous—'They began to shout out, calling for Grandier, with whom they were so much in love that the other nuns were incapable of restraining them. They wanted to go and find him and, to that end, climbed on to—and ran across—the roofs of the convent, climbed into the trees in their shifts and stood at the very ends of the branches.'

She-cats.

That the nuns are in love with the priest is something all can divine. But caterwauling in their shifts in the trees spells such disorder that the devil must have a hand in it.

The exorcisms begin immediately.

The teams follow one another in quick succession; the first exorcists, country bumpkins, are very soon exhausted. The more senior ones, brought in from the cities, don't fare much better either. In a town weakened by its three thousand dead, a formidable state machinery goes into action. Mother Jeanne des Anges' last demon eventually departs in 1637 but that's when her career as a seer begins.

As for the political background, it's clear to see. Grandier, an excellent orator and a handsome, smartly dressed man who was probably married, had written a talented pamphlet on priestly marriage, a treatise on the celibacy of priests. He was a freethinker and rebellious spirit, almost certainly hostile to the cardinal. He had had run-ins with royal justice and, though acquitted, had grown cautious.

He refused, as a result, to become spiritual advisor to the Ursuline Convent, despite pressure from the prioress (they said he was so handsome) who had never seen him. Richelieu wanted his hide and he wanted Loudun too, that fortified Protestant town which must at all costs be brought to heel. During the episodes of possession, business went on as usual—the cardinal had Loudun's ramparts razed to the ground.

Once the first period of exorcisms was over, Commissioner Jean Martin Laubardemont billeted the possessed among the townspeople, where they did embroidery. In the convent, these girls who could not be found husbands—either because they were misshapen, hunchbacked or merely unattractive (and poor, perhaps)—had lost their social status. But since they were almost all nobly born, it wasn't difficult to find homes to serve as cocoons for these black butterflies.

Twice a day they went out to the exorcisms. On their best behaviour, they marched along in single file, going off to fetch ropes and underdrawers, praying as they went. In the Sainte-Croix collegiate church, where today piano concerts are held, everything was ready for their trances.

To afford everyone a better view, the exorcists had built a raised platform by the altar steps; in the chapels, plank beds were made up with mattresses and bolsters. Straps and shackles were prepared, the ropes being brought by the nuns. One by one, they came forward as they were called to be tied up. The spectacle was about to begin. There was a large audience. Before long, nobles and princes of the blood would attend.

The curtain-raiser—handing her rosary to one of her fellow nuns, the possessed woman allowed three ropes to be knotted round her neck; she then dutifully let herself be strapped in and began to tremble as the custodial, the golden box containing the host, approached.

All the women trembled and sighed as the custodial came near. There were twenty-seven of them, possessed or 'accursed'. And their bodies were transformed.

Their eyes changed colour and their faces became contorted.

Then came the writhing. On the order of Father Lactance, the Recollect of Limoges, Jeanne des Anges turned on her stomach and raised her head while her feet and hands entwined above her back. Élisabeth Blanchard, aged nineteen, snaked towards the altar, belly uppermost, her body resting on her feet and the top of her head. And she did this so quickly that, as she climbed the two altar steps, she grasped with one hand the end of the priest's alb during the elevation. A crab.

To free the priest, Father Lactance pulled her back . . . Élisabeth threw him to the ground and beat him savagely.

As the physicians attested, pulses remained very calm. The demons alone were agitated. Blasphemies, obscenities, catcalls, unknown languages—the nun's devils were erudite and amusing, pitching jibe after jibe at the exorcists, hitting them. What a holiday was being had!

After these frenzies, they fell into a lethargy. This was the moment of inertia. They would come out of it again to 'get their rocks off'.

If the nuns required drawers, this was because their hands wanted to be at their genitals. Mme de Sazilly, a relative of Richelieu, suddenly left the communion to join her beloved Grandier. With her skirt lifted, she stuffed a crucifix into her vagina. Sister Claire's demon opened her thighs so far that her perineum touched the ground. Others stuck out their tongues in public, which were 'hard, thick, blackish, strangely long'.

They screeched and scratched, bit and yapped. Animals.

During the Second World War, American scientists, working from recordings, studied Adolf Hitler's voice as he bellowed out to immense crowds by torchlight. Whereas a normal voice produces two hundred vibrations a second when it is shouting, Hitler's went up to two hundred and twenty-eight. The power of that voice was so effective that the American agency that was later to become the CIA seriously considered slipping female hormones into the Führer's food. Aside from the staging elements—flags, drumrolls, amplifying microphones and spotlights—his speeches followed a particular method. A very long silence was followed by murmurs and whispers, then the voice rose until he was screaming. At that precise moment, women sobbed.

And men yelped.

Observing these animalistic transformations in the frenzied nuns, Father Lactance fell in with their logic. After Jeanne des Anges had assumed the acrobatic posture he ordered her to, he trampled her underfoot and placed a foot on her throat, reminding her of the words of the Psalm: 'Thou shalt tread upon the lion and adder: the young lion and the dragon shalt thou trample under feet.'

Lion, adder, young lion, dragon . . . Driven out by the exorcists and bursting forth from the nuns' mouths, their devils were often composite in nature: Asmodeus with a serpent's tail and the feet of a goose; Cerberus, a screeching crow-dog; Beelzebub, the lord of the flies, a bat with duck's feet and a lion's tail; and Hell's Lion, with the tail of a dog. This is what the nuns wanted to be—a spider with claws, an adder in the form of a crab, a flying palmiped, a bird with the body of a wildcat. During their possession and thanks to their devils, the nuns took over the bodies of fabled mythical creatures.

It's no surprise that the exorcists died. Father Lactance, who became possessed in his turn, kicked away the crucifix as the last rites were administered. Father Tranquille, his head thrown back and his arms outstretched, was tormented by a demon called Cerberus which had leapt into him from a nun. He would die a man obsessed.

The last one would meet the same fate. Four months after Grandier's final torment, Father Surin, a Jesuit, arrived, determined to speak of love.

The beatings and manhandling are set aside and a seductive approach adopted. Into the ear of Mother Jeanne des Anges he whispers Latin homilies on the inner life. The rest of the time he fasts and prays. He concerns himself with funding the nuns' allowances and accommodation costs. He feeds them and cares for them. He's the equivalent of the shaman's assistant or of those who tend to the Dakar women.

And the unthinkable occurs. Mother Jeanne des Anges recovers. Now, Father Surin is faring dreadfully—the devils have migrated. He's soon in a state of damnation, uttering the same cries 'as though they came from two different souls' and accepting all this fully. When he leaves, Jeanne des Anges is no longer possessed. Jean-Joseph Surin will be interned at Nantes, declared mad and laid low by melancholy for ten years.

How does Jeanne exit from the world of mythical beasts? The same way she entered—by a smell.

Struck down by pneumonia and deemed terminally ill by the physicians, Jeanne has a deathbed vision. The angel in the vision is barely eighteen years old and is the spitting image of François de Vendôme, Duc de Beaufort, the cousin of Louis XIV and a great womanizer who has just been to Loudun to see the exorcisms.

Jeanne sees the handsome royal prince as Saint Joseph. In her vision, the blond-wigged angel applies an ointment to her right side. She is immediately cured and on her chemise the balm leaves five drops that spread 'an admirable fragrance'.

Even more admirably, the demons have left the imprint of the names JOSEPH and MARIA on her hand in capital letters. The last demon, Behemoth, a large-bellied elephant and the personification of greed, asks to be expelled by Father Surin who is already very weak. For one last time, Jeanne goes into a trance and, on her twice-marked hand a third name appears—FRANÇOIS DE SALES. The elephant Behemoth has already flown.

The time of trances is over. The prioress receives Holy Communion once more. All that remains for her is to make a pilgrimage which quickly turns into a rock-star tour.

Offered up for popular veneration are the prioress' perfumed chemise, the cotton and the paper impregnated with the five drops of balm, together with her hand which she shows off and which the crowds adore.

In Paris, the archbishop displays the sacred hand through an open window from four in the morning until ten at night, at which point it is illuminated by torchlight. Richelieu, by now bedridden, asks to see Jeanne and observes her hand. He sniffs the chemise and kisses it, saying, 'That smells perfectly good.' At Saint-Germain-en-Laye, Queen Anne of Austria, who is pregnant, holds Jeanne's hand for more than an hour and everyone is enraptured. Some weeks later, Louis Dieudonné, the future Louis XIV, is born without mishap—this is attributed to the hand.

The fine fragrance of Jeanne's chemise is a sign. No one is in any doubt that when she dies her corpse will smell just as good and she will be hallowed on grounds of 'odour of sanctity', the fragrance of irises, violets and carnations being harbingers of an incorruptible body.

With her hand marked by divine fire, she comes in this way to be associated with the mystic nuns of the early part of her century and their mortifications: with Saint Jeanne de Chantal who, with her own hand, branded Jesus' name on her chest with hot irons; with Anne-Élisabeth de la Tulaye who carved it on her hand with a knife; with Anne-Angélique Loppin who marked it on her breasts with hot irons . . .

After this, people come to consult the prioress—about marriages, trials and to foretell the future. Jeanne has become a clairvoyant. When does this stop? Never. After her death, her head and chemise become religious relics, displayed to the public in the cause of happy pregnancies.

In retrospect, she caused a great deal of exasperation. The people of Loudun didn't appreciate the aristocrats who came as tourists, nor the noisy presentation of their town as the home of devils. In 1637, four Parisians arrived who were disinclined to believe in the posses-sions: Mlle de Rambouillet, Duchesse d'Aiguillon, Vin-cent Voiture and the abbé d'Aubignac, who would leave behind a report. The little group found numerous instances of fakery. For example, the stigmata on the hands of the prioress looked a lot like tattoos and, since they were faded and a little pale, the prioress showed them the next day red and inflamed with needle marks. D'Aubignac also saw the contortions attributed to the demon acted out with no great difficulty by one of his female friends.

The abbé d'Aubignac's conclusion was that the whole performance was merely 'deceit, fakery, abomina-tion and sacrilege'. But when the trickery was unmasked, what remained in the excellent abbé's account that was inexplicable? Those thick, black, stuck-out tongues among all the possessed.

And a sublime moment from Élisabeth Blanchard, whom the exorcist told that she must obey God because she is God's—*tu Dei es*. She replied, quick as a flash, 'To be sure, I am God.' The exorcist corrects her but Élisabeth replies with verve, 'You think I didn't hear you, but you're wrong, for you're saying that I'm God's and I'm saying that I am God.'

It is she who is right. Mystics attest to this—at Baghdad, in 922, the great Sufi al-Hallaj died on the cross for similar remarks. Writing under the pseudonym of Pierre Angélique, Georges Bataille remembered this in 1937 in *Madame Edwarda* in which the heroine, a mad prostitute, exposes her vulva for veneration with the same words.

Loudun found it very hard to recover from the stuck-out tongues and the girls turned into God through the good offices of demons.

Though supposed a witch by her neighbours, Marie Besnard didn't stick out her tongue. In 1949, on the strength of rumours, the 'Good Lady of Loudun' was accused of poisoning twelve people with arsenic. Successive trials having failed to prove the case, she was acquitted in 1961. While following the Marie Besnard affair, the court reporter Frédéric Pottecher made the comparison between the accusations of witchcraft against Grandier and those against Besnard four centuries later in the same town of Loudun. The defendant had no particular distinguishing marks, except her voice—'a little girl's voice'.

But a silvery voice in a grown woman's body—that's not nothing.

The possessed today are singers of both sexes who offer up their tattooed muscles, their bound, corseted bodies, their boots, sweat and exhaustion for public veneration. The trances are in the auditorium—and sometimes on the stage.

Joy Sorman is describing Joey Starr of the rappers NTM in concert—'Joey's body on stage toppling, swivelling, jerking; his crippled piston of a body, mounted on ball bearings, left hanging by the "scratch" effect, its movement first suspended, then picking up again epileptically. With a series of breaks and suspensions, he thrashes around like a madman, writhes as a croaking shakes his body, laughs until he cries. This isn't the spectacle of a man in a trance but a commitment to performance, a giving of himself.'

And yet you'd have to describe it as a trance—'Joey is all animals: buzzard, puma, falcon, jaguar, bear, hyena, stuck pig. He knows all their noises. Joey Starr is a menagerie.'

But no, not a trance. Just its representation. 'Give the audience its money's worth,' says Joy Sorman in this story which she entitled 'Noise'.

CHAPTER 6

A-e-i-o-u
(Paris and Outreau, Northern France)

Moving on one century in France, when the trance of witchcraft and sorcery disappears, it returns under another name.

The great French epidemic had begun in the early years of the seventeenth century. Before Loudun, first the Basque country, then Aix and Marseilles had been hit by witchcraft. After Loudun, it was the turn of Louviers and Chinon. The provincial *parlements* competed to condemn the most witches. The slightest suspicion sufficed.

In 1670, in the Béarn, a fifteen-year-old apprentice announced he could identify any sorceror by a black mark on the face visible only to him. He began in June on Midsummer's Day. By November, he'd identified six thousand two hundred. The *parlement* of Pau, capital of the Béarn, prosecuted them zealously.

In 2001, at Outreau, west of Boulogne, a young examining magistrate began the investigation of a case of paedophilia, following a procedure that is termed 'inquisitorial'.

In the role of apprentice or of Jeanne des Anges, a woman under suspicion of incest and paedophilia made accusations against a 'network' of seventeen people and even informed the police of the murder of a little girl, indicating the place where the body was buried. Nothing was found at the spot.

In the role of Urbain Grandier we had abbé Dominique Wiel, a former farmhand, a soldier during the Algerian civil war turned worker-priest, a Communist sympathizer living in the same building as the woman levelling the main accusations.

In the role of the exorcists, social workers from France's Child Welfare Services and official psychological experts. In the role of the provincial *parlements*, the officers of the Saint-Omer law courts.

All those presumed innocent were immediately incarcerated. At the end of the trial, the priest received the heaviest sentence—a seven-year prison term. On appeal, the woman broke down and announced she had been lying. The children did the same. Thirteen of those convicted were acquitted. They had spent between three and four years in prison. For nothing.

Brought face to face with his accuser, as is the practice in French law, abbé Dominique Wiel, horrified at the way the investigation was being conducted, rose to his feet and sang the *Marseillaise*. 'An unforgettable scene' then unfolded—the accuser first fell to her knees weeping, then crawled on all fours to take refuge behind the young magistrate.

On all fours!

In 1671, six months after the Pau affair, Jean-Baptiste Colbert gave the order to suspend all proceedings and the Pau *parlement* complied, its magistrates having lined their pockets during the commissions of inquiry and one of the commissions' members having induced the sorcerer's apprentice to make mass accusations for financial reasons. That same year, in the town of Condom, a boy of fourteen identified sorcerers 'for free' and was arrested.

The royal edict of 1682 put an end to prosecutions for witchcraft. And, to begin with, it ordered a general expulsion of 'bohemians' and fortune tellers.

Even in those days . . .

From 1682 onwards, claiming to be a witch or warlock was outlawed; offenders, deemed 'false sorcerers', would be imprisoned or interned at la Salpêtrière asylum in Paris. The devil had lost. The provincial *parlements*, with their financial stake in accusations of witchcraft, had lost too. Where would trances migrate to now?

To a cemetery in Paris.

In 1711, Louis XIV ordered the abbey of Port-Royal-des-Champs to be destroyed. It was the mecca for Jansenist retreats, a place dedicated to grace which alone was regarded as capable of saving the sinner. The highly popular Jansenists carried on a great many charitable activities and dispensed education to the poor in a spirit of asceticism and humility.

The abbey, which was frequented by the Solitaires—the 'Gentlemen' who lived strictly austere lives in little houses set apart—took in veterans of the Fronde (the religious civil wars of 1648–53) who, even in retirement, continued to contest the king's power in a low-key way. No trance without an adjacent rebellion.

And then the abbey was razed to the ground. For Port-Royal gave rise to miracle cures. Port-Royal had the corpses of the 'Gentlemen'—those corpses exuding the odour of sanctity—cut into little pieces, and these little bits of flesh and bone turned into efficacious relics. Divine grace. And it is sufficient.

Louis XIV opened the tombs and had the bones removed to other sites.

The Jansenist remains were taken, within Paris, to Saint-Jacques-du-Haut-Pas (those of the abbé of Saint-Cyran and Mme de Longueville), Saint-Étienne du Mont (those of Racine, Boileau and Pascal), Saint-Séverin, Saint-Eustache and Saint-Médard—parishes open to Jansenist spirituality and hence in revolt against authority.

In 1713, Pope Clement XI published the bull *Unigenitus*, denouncing the Jansenist theses as 'suspected of, and savouring of, heresy'. An immediate polemic ensued. In its battle with the king and the papacy, Jansenism became a popular cause.

François de Pâris, the eldest son of a father who was one of the 'nobles of the robe', declined the hereditary office that would have come to him, preferring to enter the church. To obtain a vicarship, he had, in accordance with the pastoral letters, to sign a 'formulary' by which he committed himself personally against Jansenism.

Pâris didn't want to sign. Moreover, acting from a sense of conscience, he didn't even accept the vicarship that was offered to him in a spirit of conciliation. It was a 'no'—he was a Jansenist. He would not be a vicar; he would be a deacon.

He devoted himself to the poor. He lived with them and as they did. He ate almost nothing and lived in a cabin. He became a stockinger. He sold his furniture, giving away the money and his clothes. Against his skin, he wore garters and bracelets of pointed iron chain. Lively and charismatic but afflicted with tremors, he lived in the parish of Saint-Médard in the Faubourg Saint-Marcel. And died in his cabin in 1727 at the age of thirty-seven.

Deacon Pâris' body is barely cold when the miracles begin to happen. A silk winder rubs her paralysed arm against his bier and it is healed. Within a day, the poor of the district have cut up his mattress and the last stocking he wove. A tree begins to grow near the spot where he's been buried according to his wishes—'without funeral hangings, ringing of bells or lighting of candles'. The tree is quickly cut to pieces.

To protect the body, his family erects a tomb—four supports surmounted by a slab of black marble.

Perfect for lying on.

On the tomb, people go into convulsions, particularly women. Pain comparable to that of giving birth, as they put it, tears out their entrails and cracks their joints. Their bones are dislocated; they writhe and scream. Since there are loggias in the cemetery, the spectacle begins above the graves. The upper classes make their appearance, of course, as at Loudun. Miracles are heaped one upon the other, with encouragement from the Jansenist curés.

In July 1731, the archbishop of Paris orders a woman claiming to have been cured by a miracle to be examined by physicians. They find she has suffered a fit of hysteria. She is officially denied miracle status.

Six days later, Aimée Pivert, a forty-two-year-old servant, suffering from paralysis and tremors, 'goes into convulsions' on the black marble slab, shaking so violently that her bones are heard to crack.

The convulsions don't stop when she comes down from the slab. The symptoms haven't disappeared but Aimée is declared healed. This is the first turning point.

After Aimée, convulsions are taken as the sign of an imminent cure. Soon they'll be the equivalent of a cure.

Geneviève, who has trouble with her eyes, nose and ears, finds she's described as 'completely recovered', though she still can't hear and hasn't lost her cough. Barbe, who has a crippled foot, is cured, though her ankle hasn't recovered at all, she says. Marie, a hunchback, experiences convulsions and emerges still a hunchback—or, in other words, cured. What matter that nothing has changed? She went into convulsions, didn't she?

Cure isn't what this is really about. It's about ecstasy and nothing more.

An old-clothes seller provided 'leading strings' free of charge to tie up the women, who are 'getting their rocks off' here, heads hanging down on the black marble. These leading strings were important—all the women would be trussed up in bondage gear. Their arms and breasts were naked, their skirts raised, their legs vertical. The assistants practised a form of active aid known as 'succour'.

We have reached the nub of the matter.

A *mouche* (a policeman in 'civvies') reports in December, 'The most scandalous thing is to see pretty, shapely girls in the arms of men who, as they succour them, are able to satisfy certain passions . . . As happened to me when I tried to perform the same service for the girl who put her two feet on my shoulders and whose thighs remained uncovered.' We can imagine the scene. At one end of the grave the girl is quivering, head hung down and feet on the policeman's shoulders, thighs open and no drawers.

Drawers were provided.

In January 1732, the king had the Saint-Médard cemetery closed. Two hundred 'Convulsionaries' had lain on the tomb. They were common, not high born, people—'people of no consequence, peasant women, servant girls, working women', as an anonymous text had it. The dangerous classes! As he actually did say of witches, Michelet would have said that the Convulsionaries came from 'the times of despair'.

At this point, convulsion went over into resistance.

Six months later—she's been betrayed to the authorities—we find Angélique Grasset on the third floor of a wine merchant's. She has six people sit on her, has herself trampled on, shaken, thrown in the air.

But this is just a beginning. There follows a yanking on breasts—two women each pull on one of the breasts of Sister Françoise—Françoise Obillard—while, to help them pull harder, two men pull on each of the two women. 'Tear it off,' shouts the Convulsionary.

Then come the logs and the sword thrusts. Logs are piled on bodies as if for a cremation; swords are thrust against the flesh, throats dug into, bodies crushed. Without penetrating the skin? The 'belabourings' leave bruises but don't shed blood.

For the moment. Things remain for now within the bounds of a rather rough initiation.

In *The Elementary Forms of Religious Life*, Émile Durkheim, writing in 1912, lists examples of pain inflicted on novices during the initiations of Australian aborigines. Among the Larakia, those overseeing the rite surprise the initiates with violent blows while they are on retreat in the bush; among the Urabunna, the novice lies on the ground, his face to the earth, and receives blows from all the men present, who cut his back—four to eight cuts—then place one cut in the middle of the back of his neck; among the Arunta, the novice is thrown in the air, caught and thrown up again . . . These are highly defined rituals, practised and endured very determinedly in order to integrate an initiate into adult life.

But the Convulsionaries invent their rituals as they go along. Clearly, that will never be good enough. Let's attend to Daniel Vidal, the best of their scribes, describing the miracles and convulsions.

Sister Crosse receives two thousand 'blows from the sword' and, a few days later, another thousand. And is struck as many times with logs. Tokens of this 'succour' are printed and distributed for the defence of popular faith, giving rise to a remarkable degree of emulation. More and more indeed.

Girls hold their faces to the fire, the intensity of which is tested by having an egg and cutlets cook as they hang from the willing victim's neck. The cutlets cook and the eggs harden. The girl's faces remain unharmed. Yet this isn't enough!

One day, the swords penetrate into the flesh.

And when they come to the end of the swords, the logs and the flames, they go back finally to the reference myth, to Jesus on the Cross. Yet it isn't the cross that's of interest but the piercing nails.

One person doesn't just ask for a single crucifixion but for several in a single day. Examined by Dr Morand, a member of the Academy of Medicine, Sister Félicité was crucified so many times that she had calluses on her feet and hands. Under Dr Morand's eyes, the crucified Convulsionary showed no sign of pain, speaking merrily as she turned her head to right and left to see her interlocutors. She bled very little. They took her down from the cross.

It was at that point that she asked 'Papa' to pierce her tongue.

Who was Papa? Monsieur François-Jean de la Barre, leader of a particularly active group, who pierced, nailed and struck for all they were worth. And Papa did as he was asked, taking a stylet and splitting the tongue cross-wise. The doctor saw everything but didn't intervene.

Did the women die? Inevitably.

In 1755, Sister Françoise—the same one—asked to be 'succoured' by Father Cottu who scrupulously kept the register of these actions. Blows from logs, chains and hammers; tongues drawn with pincers, then hammered; arrows shot into their sides; peppered with sword thrusts; rolled in a barrel full of razor blades, knives and nails. In 1760, having been stoned, buried alive, crucified and crushed, Sister Françoise died in odour of sanctity after being nailed to a wall by five sword thrusts. Her last words: 'Everything comes to an end. Here at last is the great convulsion.'

In January 1789, six months before the storming of the Bastille, Marguerite Bernard died after a last pilgrimage to the site where Port-Royal-des-Champs had been razed to the ground—she had walked there with nails in her feet.

Yes, inevitably they died. In the meantime, the convulsions were accompanied by strange 'infancies'.

Since there are 'papas', there will also be little girls stubbornly speaking baby-talk—something Jacques Lacan recognized as a sign of the most serious disturbances. For this infantile speech isn't a regression to the future anterior through which one constructs one's memory in a psychoanalytic cure, but a mark of delirium.

Madelon, a lady's maid: 'Papa want to mould my little brother. Papa you wants to put him into this pen. Papa told me this child will become like a little animal.' *As what* is Madelon raving about the child, the little animal 'Papa' is going to put into his pen? As a nanny-goat, to give birth to a devilish kid, or as a ewe, to bring forth a divine lamb?

The succourer's remarks: 'Come and take care of these children, come and instruct them, Lord, and have them say, like little children, a-e-i-o-u. Yes, Lord! Oh, how happy they will be! This is where all knowledge lies. Come then and loosen their tongues to have them endlessly repeat a-e-i-o-u. Never allow those who come with fury and corruption in their hearts to pronounce distinctly a-e-i-o-u. Turn and destroy their tongues . . .'

There will even be a paedophilic version: the fifteen-month-old Louison suffers convulsions and tongue injuries while rolling round his mouth a little silver cross, because someone put it there.

The tongue an object of desire. Split, roasted, studded, stuck out fat and blackened, this tortured tongue will be capable of speaking the 'mother of languages', the innocent language of Paradise.

So it is with initiations in the vodun of Benin, in Haitian voodoo and in candomblé at Salvador de Bahia. In these, the simulation of a return to childhood is obligatory. So too is death, but only faked. For in a managed initiation, the initiates do not die; they are reborn, transformed. A real trance doesn't kill.

Unless it's being used, as is the case in sati.

There was a time in India when a widow saw it as her duty to allow herself to be burnt alive with her dead husband, thus becoming a sati. This wasn't so long ago. Roop Kanwar, the last identified sati, burnt in 1987 in the state of Rajasthan. According to the *Times of India*, another woman is said to have performed the act in 2008.

This voluntary sacrifice has to be validated by the Brahman authorities who verify that the widow isn't menstruating, isn't pregnant and has made the decision freely. Sometimes a widow puts a flaming candle against the skin of her arm to show her determination. But why? And how can it be that a woman wants to be burnt alive?

Society promises her she will become a goddess, attracting all kinds of benefits to the group. The surviving widow was secretly regarded as responsible for the husband's death and was for many years mistreated by his family. She was deprived of salt, spices, holidays and new saris and reduced to a state of servitude.

But divine glory and the fear of ill-treatment wouldn't be sufficient if the rite didn't also involve a sort of inversion of the powers of the flame; it wouldn't burn or inflict pain but envelop the body like 'a cooling bath'. Leaving her body behind in the coolness of the fire, the woman on the pyre would find another immortal, radiant, eternally feminine one.

Driven on and supported by the group and its chanting, the widow ascended the pyre in her wedding sari, dressed in red, bejewelled, her face painted, triumphant. And in a trance. This is what an old Indian woman friend explained to me when the young widow burnt in Rajasthan.

Forced? No. Group pressure and the promise that the flames would be like a cooling bath, together with the trance induced by the extraordinary collective excitation—that was enough.

A number of hitherto progressive Indian intellectuals defended the sati principle, as did the Indian nationalist extreme Right in the name of the values of Hinduism.

But the trance cannot be accepted when it kills.

In France, in the twenty-first century, death is toyed with in private places where not just anyone can play. Those charged with providing the 'succour', the dominators or dominatrixes, who define themselves as sex workers, dispense pleasure—and perhaps also love—in secure BDSM 'dungeons'. Whatever the strictures applied to the client's body, a code word is agreed on to halt these as soon as a signal is given. 'Pax!' and the game is ended. The 'leading strings' of the Saint-Médard cemetery's 'succourers' have turned into a complex arrangement of bonds requiring trust and extreme caution (no slipknots, the bondagee is not to be left alone, restraint is to be shown where there's visible pain, etc.).

These—consensual—tortures resemble the 'succour' requested by the Convulsionaries, though there are three differences and they are important: the dominators are providing a service for money; divine grace is not systematically invited into these ceremonies; and barring accidents, no one dies.

The French exceptionalism where the Convulsionaries are concerned lies in the fact that they actually died. This wasn't playing, it was killing. Why do we have the impression that the Convulsionaries were attempting shamanism without proper training? Because they died, that's why.

Animal commotions. The woman Lopin, known as Sister Barker, barked like a bulldog and chewed the cud like a cow; Brother Pierre barked for two hours a day; Louis roared like a lion; Anne bellowed like a bull; at Saint-Pignans, they howled like wolves. Everywhere, they vomited and foamed at the mouth. And since they were dogs, they ate excrement. 'God is found amid all that is most corrupt and vile,' cried Brother Ottin.

And, consequently, Sister Auguste, known as the Stercophage, began, after strict fasting, to eat human excrement, doing so for twenty-one days, mingling it at times with urine and spicing it with soot, hair, nail parings, snot and earwax.

And now came something new. Once she had digested all this, there flowed from her lips a delicious milk which was gathered in cups and consumed devoutly by the witnesses to the scene.

Soon the Convulsionaries would be totally naked and blind drunk; they would be sacred prostitutes. The Church having lost its usefulness, Marie Durié took the definitive step and committed the truly great sacrilege, the only one to cause scandal and amazement—she celebrated Mass, dispensing Communion, filling a chalice with wine and passing it round. Now, for a woman to act the priest is far worse than death.

These bodily changes, these holy transgressions were accompanied by accounts of visions.

As good shamanesses, the women had, in the end, to utter prophecies. In April 1787, Sister Aile announced, 'The Revolution must take place . . . I see only ambushes, I see only precipices, I hear the sound of arms. The king's palace is swept away, his crown is taken from him.'

This is 'the great convulsion'.

We have no archives on this from the days of the Revolution. 'In certain historical periods, under the influence of some great collective upheaval, social interactions become more frequent and more active,' writes Durkheim in *The Elementary Forms of Religious Life*. 'Individuals seek each other out and assemble more often. The result is a general effervescence characteristic of revolutionary or creative epochs. Now, this hyperactivity has the effect of generally stimulating individual energies. People live differently and more intensely than in normal times. The changes are not only those of nuance and degree; man himself becomes other.'

The change occurred. Yes, the poor prophetesses—these 'nobodies'—were right. They foresaw the future.

The Paris Jansenists, hostile to the Church of France and to the papacy, approved the Civil Constitution of the Clergy passed by the Constituent Assembly in July 1790. Ecclesiastics became for a time state employees; bishops and priests were elected; the Church of France became wholly independent of the papacy and abbeys and monasteries were to disappear.

Abbé Grégoire, well known for his attachment to the Jansenist spirit of Port-Royal-des-Champs, a friend of the freemasons and a member for the clergy in the Estates-General, had a hand in drawing up the Civil Constitution of the Clergy. This is the same abbé Grégoire who had slavery abolished and introduced Jews into the national community of France.

At one end of the scale, the cruelty of 'succour' rains down on consenting girls; at the other, philosophical liberty accompanies a kind of perfect ideal of humanism.

In 1807, the intact skeleton of François de Pâris was exhumed and his twenty-eight teeth shared out. Was the long convulsion over at last? Not quite.

A converted Jew, Félicité Boussin, known as Sister Isaac, was a member of a network of Convulsionaries. During the Revolution, unlike abbé Grégoire, Sister Isaac campaigned against the juring clergy[1] and later, under the Empire, against the signing of the Concordat and the pope who accepted it. Neither state nor pope. Her only Church was Jansenism.

She lived at Lyon in a trance. The archives depict her as imbued with a powerful cadaverous odour; she could keep no food down and vomited putrescence.

---

1 Those committed to the Civil Constitution of the Clergy—Trans.

What did she say? That God, abhorring 'the guilty, impious and ungrateful Gentiles', was preparing to call the people of Israel back to him. When does she say these words? In 1825.

And on the same day: 'Since the return of the Jews will be, for the Church, like a resurrection from among the dead, the Jews will therefore work in the Church to make all as it was before.' In 1837, she was still uttering prophecies.

CHAPTER 7

The Little Animal

The girls you see screaming and waving their arms in the air at the feet of singers are often called 'hysterical'. Hysterical fans.

Like the *coup de foudre*, this adjective, which has entered everyday parlance, has a particular pedigree. The term 'hysteric'—an offshoot of the sorcerer's trance and the convulsions of Saint-Médard and also the soil from which, around the year 1900, psychoanalysis emerged—is a classic one in psychiatry. Though it has come down in the world to refer to what Paul Valéry in 'Le Cimetière marin' called 'the shrill cries of tickled girls' ('les cris aigus des filles chatouillées'),[2] the term seems indestructible.

An example. In 1925, in France, when Freudian thought was first beginning to make inroads, the Stock Publishing House issued a little book by Dr Jean Vinchon, former director of a clinic and assistant professor at the University of Paris, as part of a series of educational works under the general heading 'Modern Culture'. Its title: *Hysteria*.

Its contents were clear—since antiquity, there had been an alliance between sex and animality. Take the following observation by Galen, a Greek physician from Pergamum in the third century CE: a midwife called out

2 Cecil Day-Lewis translates charmingly but very freely as 'The bird-sharp cries of girls whom love is teasing.'—Trans.

to treat a hysteric massaged her womb, bringing from it 'a plentiful, thick liquid' which was expelled with 'a mixture of pain and pleasure, a sensation comparable to that accompanying sexual relations'. The masturbation of a fountain-woman.

Stranger than this were the noises made by women in trances. Burps, farts, intestinal rumblings, piercing cries, sobs, tears, outbursts of laughter. Everything that's improper in polite society bursts out for everyone to hear. The daughters of the governor of Rouen were seized with violent—and rebellious—laughter for a whole hour. Voices welled up from viscera, imitating 'the cawing of the crow, the hissing of the snake, the crowing of the cockerel or the dog's howl'. We're back with chimaeras again.

The other strand is one of inertia, if not indeed of apparent death, which was for a long time a source of terror. Catalepsy, immobilized muscles, bodies turned to statues, corpse-like life. In India, they say that yogis, who have entered a state of voluntary catalepsy, have been buried for a month—locked up in chests, under surveillance—and come out alive. Catalepsy, giving the outward appearance of death, is a silence of the organs, the merest murmur of life, with the heart operating in slow motion.

In both cases—noise and silence—the assumption has been that the problem comes from the uterus, that little animal living within women's bodies and capable of leaping from the genitals to the throat. The travelling uterus has a purpose. In moving, in rising from the vagina to the mouth, it is rejecting its function and resolving not to produce children.

To this end, Ambroise Paré tells us, 'The uterus swells and inflates and is, hence, seized and carried upwards by a forced and, as it were, convulsive movement on account of the plenitude of its vessels.'

We have been warned—the little animal is itself in a trance. It isn't the woman who's carried away—it's her womb.

It has direct purchase on the nostrils. When no longer suffocating, the woman sneezes. This marks the end of the crisis.

Paré's treatments included the following: laying the woman down, unlacing her clothing, shouting her name into her ears and, at the same time, pulling on her pubic hair to hold her womb in place. Jérôme Cardan advocates use of the powdered hooves of the elk, an animal one wouldn't expect to find in these parts.

All make use of aromas. Good aromas: musk, civet, amber and angelica which is similar to musk; fetid aromas: burnt horn. The women aren't just made to smell the aromas with their nostrils, but these are also placed in proximity to their nether regions, directly into the nose of the little animal. And the woman sneezes.

A century later, the belief in the little animal that leaps into the throat is gone. Mme de Cligny, a patient of Dr Pierre Pomme, has been bedridden for twenty-seven years—since the first year of her marriage—on account of convulsive leg tremors, cramps and vertigo. Dr Pomme, the author of *Essai sur les affections vaporeuses des deux sexes contenant une nouvelle méthode de traiter ces maladies* published in 1760, treats her with water: enemas, drinking, hot and tepid baths and, in particular, an eight-hour cool bath. After ten months, Pomme unhesitatingly declares the patient cured and orders her to travel. She leaves her bed and does so.

Mme de Cligny is by this point fifty years old; in that era, the time for sex was past for women.

On the eve of the Revolution, while crucified girls are prophesying the death of the king, women are having the vapours around the *baquet* of Mesmer the Austrian, who strokes them with his iron rod in front of his assistants in magnetism, the *valets toucheurs*, who gather up the vapourish women in their trances.

They have to be seen. They have to be touched.

Paris in the 1880s, half a century after the prophecies of Sister Isaac, the Convulsionary of Lyon. In a lecture theatre at la Salpêtrière hospital, Professor Jean-Baptiste Charcot is producing a medical spectacle, freeing up paralysed women under hypnosis, women whose symptoms return as soon as they're awakened. Charcot, entirely aware of reproducing the scenes of exorcisms and of the Convulsionaries when he classified the phases of hysteria, strung together the 'epileptoid phase' which paralyses, the phase of 'clownism' or contortions, the phase of 'emotional outbursts' with its supplications and ecstasies, the 'terminal period' of relief and smiling, and added a 'demonic variety of hysteria' with hallucinations. Not forgetting the so-called cynical spasm which provides a marvellous simulation of orgasm.

Cynical here means having no sense of modesty, like a dog.

Freud was in the audience. And, most important, he heard what Charcot said repeatedly—namely, that this inexplicable phenomenon had a traumatic cause and, in every case, 'genital matters' are 'always, always involved'.

The cause is in the vagina. There's nothing new under the sun.

With Josef Breuer, Freud treated hysterics. He was very wary of them. In Vienna, these young middle-class sorceresses behaved reasonably well—no writhing about, no sticking out of tongues. But the troubles they were suffering from were like a distant echo of the scenes of possession. Tongues, throats, voices, demons, odours.

Katharina, an innkeeper's niece who had lived in the city, sees a terrifying male face and feels she's suffocating.

Lucy, the housekeeper of a rich entrepreneur, suffers from horrific olfactory sensations and a recurrent cold.

Emmy, the wife of a leading industrialist, who feels a monster with a vulture's beak pecking at her stomach, unexpectedly makes bird noises, involving the clicking of her tongue in a way reminiscent of the mating cry of the male coot.

Dora suffers from hoarseness, losses of voice and spasmodic fainting. Later will come the white wolves sitting on the tree, Little Hans' horse and the sodomizing rat in the bestiary of the five case histories.

Visions of terrifying men in the night, haunting smells, animal cries, vulture-like monsters and transformed voices—Freud's well brought up hysterics aren't far removed at all from their forerunners in the nunneries and the forests.

Instead of maltreating them by forcing a round, gilded box on to abusive lips, Freud has their mouths speak. Since the hysterics are suffering from 'reminiscences', these must be transformed into stored memories. Manufacturing a memory—in the best of cases, language work replaces the symptom by the recounting of a lost memory.

The question of whether that memory is true or false, which weighed on Freud's mind for a long time, is no more important than the question of simulation; the key thing is the coherence of the account and the emotion it releases. Though the end of the crisis isn't a sneeze, it does lie in something almost negligible. For example, in deportment.

For instance, Lucy arrives one day smiling and with her head held upright, rather than leaning stubbornly to one side. Lucy, for so long in love with her employer, had come now to think there was no future for her love but also that this didn't matter much. All things considered, she was free to feel as she wished. At the end of *Studies on Hysteria*, Freud stated something that seemed to him self-evident—that the treatment consisted in transforming 'hysterical misery into common unhappiness'.

No more.

And no less.

The crisis can also resolve itself in a waltz. Elisabeth, a young aristocrat, constantly walks with the upper part of her body leaning forward on account of unexplained muscle pains. In Elisabeth's case, the therapist eschews hypnosis and the analysis begins. An account of the trauma is offered—Elisabeth, who is in love with a boy, feels very guilty since the time when, returning from an outing with her beau, she had found her father in a critical state.

The analysis was a very long one, but one spring day the therapist learnt that Elisabeth was going to one of the last balls of Fasching, the Viennese carnival. He got himself invited, since, he says, 'I did not allow the opportunity to escape me of seeing my former patient whirl past in a lively dance.' The rebellion was transformed from hysterical misery into the pleasure of the waltz.

The scene is incredible. The frock-coated therapist contentedly observes a young woman waltzing—or perhaps being whirled around in the wild galop that begins at 2 a.m. at the Fasching balls.

She no longer feels pain in her back; she is galloping. A young foal.

CHAPTER 8

Dracula's Daughters
(Ireland; USA)

Eighteen ninety-seven. Two years after the appearance of *Studies on Hysteria*, the Irishman Bram Stoker published *Dracula*, a fantasy novel which was an overnight success.

For centuries the vampire had had his place in Europe. Britain, Austria, Hungary, Serbia, Moravia and Silesia had, successively, seen cases of the living dead. Stoker placed him in Romania and made him a descendant of Vlad Tepes, known as 'Vlad the Impaler', prince of Wallachia.

'Dracula' means 'son of Dracul', dragon or devil. He is a hero of a chimaerical order. Like Zeus before him, the vampire-count can turn into a wolf, a rat, a bat or mere dust flittering about in a ray of light. He crawls like a lizard over the walls of his castle, flies off, disappears. Recognizable by the hairs on his palms and his stinking breath, Count Dracula is an elegant smooth-talker, assisted by gypsies. It had to be gypsies.

We know the vampire's survival principle—fresh blood drunk by night. By day he recuperates, inert in his coffin. He is immortal. But vulnerable—he thirsts for blood.

Though Dracula may, if pressed, drink animal blood, he prefers to suck from the throats of young women. When it is Stoker doing the writing, his British victims are kindly middle-class girls, bold, feminist and educated. The first of them, Lucy, will become a vampire. Thanks to hypnosis, the second, Minna, narrowly manages to escape his clutches. A sleepwalker, Lucy belongs to the cohort of the age's hysterics, shifting from laughter to melancholy even as she pursues her vampiric activity of sucking children's blood.

She will be a daughter of Dracula.

A strange enigma! The vampire needs a family. If he has his devoted followers, held in thrall like a sect-member by a modern guru, Dracula 'has' women in order to procreate daughters. No vaginal penetration, no sperm. The vampire penetrates through the arteries. The erogenous zones are limited to necks and breasts; things don't go any lower.

This assisted procreation is a thing of great purity; there's nothing dirty about it. Dracula's daughters aren't born *inter faeces et urinas*, between shit and urine, as Saint Augustine had it. They're born cleanly.

In Transylvania, there are already three of them, chatty and coaxing. Attractive girls who enjoy a laugh. Ah, that laughter—'a silvery, musical laugh, but as hard as though the sound never could have come through the softness of human lips. It was like the intolerable, tingling sweetness of water glasses when played on by a cunning hand.'

It's a sound we find in other trance scenes— candomblé initiates in Bahia are awakened and sent back to the dance by a little bell tinkled gently beside their ears. When separated from Iseult, Tristan has her hold a little dog whose collar contains an enchanted little bell that revives love. The laughter of Dracula's daughters is musical in nature—it is a glockenspiel.

A little girl's laughter, like the curious voice of Marie Besnard, the 'Good Lady of Loudun'.

Now, at the end of Lucy's funeral, the exorcist-in-chief, the stern Professor Van Helsing, succumbs to a fit of crazed laughter. Laughter, perturbing and short-circuiting the mind, is a little trance; it is uncontrollable, coming in involuntary bursts and clouding the brain.

There's a reason for this laughter. Before the open grave, Lucy's fiancé solemnly proclaims that, having given his blood in a transfusion, she remains his wife for all eternity. But this blood relationship is somewhat confused. Van Helsing reminds him that, since other men also gave the girl their blood, the dead Lucy is a polygamist . . . At this idea, the professor is seized by an attack of wild laughter. And he is right.

The strength of the vampire—the reason why he works his magic—is that, by escaping death, he invents another form of relationship. The vampire creates a world without any eclipse, a world in which the idea of rest does not apply. A world that has ceased to rebel.

There's only one exception in Stoker's novel. Dracula has just reprimanded his—laughing—daughters who were guilty of trying to suck the blood of one of his victims. They accuse him of an inability to love. 'Yes, I too can love; you yourselves can tell it from the past. Is it not so?'

Through the tiny door of an imposing vampire's capacity for love has flooded the current fashion for vampires—these generous souls—big-hearted knights errant—these baby vampires who find a protector, these cruel girls who don't grow up—a whole host of characters to rouse the passions of adolescents just as their bodies are changing and becoming capable of procreation.

The year 2005 saw the beginning of the publication in the USA of the *Twilight* series, the work of a very young author Stephenie Meyer, which achieved stunning success among high-school students. Four volumes tell the story of the wild passion between a pale young girl and a handsome seventeen-year-old vampire with copper-coloured hair and dark rings round his eyes.

It begins in high school, in cloakrooms and classrooms and at the end-of-year hop.

A 'grand hysteric', Bella faints with great regularity, stumbles over, dreams, falls into trances. She harbours a violent desire to be a vampire, eager to know all she can about them. Edward, her vampire boyfriend, loves her with Kantian scruples, obsessed as he is by the fear he may hurt her—the new monsters are changed creatures.

Like the vampires of old, they are endowed with second sight, telepathic powers and irresistible strength. And they run so fast that they fly up into the air. When sight alone fails them, they sniff things out, using their highly developed sense of smell. Nothing new so far, then.

But the sunshine doesn't kill them—they sparkle in it. Their breath is scented rather than stinking. They don't have fangs but the shiniest white teeth. Their skin verges on alabaster and is hard as stone. They never sleep, particularly not in the daytime, for by day they hunt. Animals only.

As respecters of human rights, these modern vampires don't suck the blood of humans. That imposes a great strain, since they would like to. But the vampire who's in love, a very well-mannered young man, comes of a strict family. His father is a hospital doctor—unstinting through thick and thin—and his children have been brought up to act with compassion.

The fact remains, however, that they were 'created' in the old style by way of lethal love bites. The father was bitten in London during one of the great plagues. To build himself a family, he rescued dying people. For example, Bella's boyfriend was created as he was dying from Spanish flu in 1919. Biting human beings is taboo, except when death is approaching and they have to be rescued.

Good American that he is, the amorous vampire marries the girl with the pale complexion. There is, then, a wedding: flowery canopy, wedding rings, presents, a wedding dress. There will be a wedding night, though we won't be told much about it, except that vampires now have a sexuality that reaches below the belt.

This is something new. Vampires make the beast with two backs.

And the beast is a violent one. The young bride awakens with her body covered in bruises. Very soon she is pregnant. This wasn't anticipated. The foetus grows at lightning speed and the birth goes horribly wrong. To save the child, its father will open the mother's belly with his vampire teeth, for the womb is as solid as stone. And, since she's dying, her husband will practice the Great Transformation on Bella.

But in a modern way. Under medical surveillance he injects his vampire blood into her heart, taking care to administer morphine too since the transformation is immensely painful.

When she awakens, Bella has an entirely new voice, a voice that is silvery like a clinking of glasses. And she has a daughter.

At this point, so much aspired to, where human and animal intermingle, we have before us a girl born of a vampire father and a human mother.

From high school to marriage, the lovers have conformed, then, to the average American ideal and will end up 'starting a family'. The exception with the little *Twilight* family is that they'll live for ever. With death not on the horizon, there's no need for an eclipse. The hysteric is cured.

By night Bella will go hunting for puma. By day she feeds her child from a bottle of blood.

CHAPTER 9

The *Tarantati* of Apulia
(Southern Italy)

The heel of the Italian 'boot'—Puglia in Italian—is called Apulia in English and is famous for its *trulli*, dwellings with flat-stone roofs. The roofs have magical signs on them, painted in whitewash. At Tarento, in Apulia, there has been since 1989 a festival aimed at revitalizing the traditional music scene. On the poster, a crescent moon shines down on a giant spider.

Thirty years before this, Ernesto de Martino, a professor of the history of religion, went out into the ancient territory of Apulia to study a celebrated musical trance phenomenon named Tarantism.

The facts have been studied since the late Middle Ages. Leonardo da Vinci left a brief note on the subject and, in the sixteenth century, some called Apulia 'the Indies of the Abruzzi' because of the strangeness of this type of possession. Father Athanasius Kircher, a German Jesuit, who invented the megaphone and, it is said, a piano made up of cats whose tails, when crushed, produced mewing that ran from bass to treble, was one of those to take an interest in the phenomenon. To follow up their efforts, De Martino formed a multidisciplinary team which included a psychiatrist, a psychologist, a social worker, a sociologist and a musicologist. In 1961, he published *La Terra del rimorso: Contributo a una storia religiosa del Sud—The Land of Remorse: A Study of Southern Italian Tarantism*.

In Apulia, in 1959, people were bitten by spiders known as tarantulas. Their poisonous sting produced headaches, dizziness, depression, fatigue, fever and delirium. The syndrome often returned the following year on the anniversary of the first bite. The tarantula bit its victims a second time, more than eighty-five per cent of them being women, of course.

As far as spiders are concerned, there are two poisonous insects in Apulia: the *Lycosa*, a nasty brown hairy spider whose bite causes a painful swelling which has no effect on the rest of the body; and the *Latrodectus*, a smaller, less conspicuous creature, whose bite is painless but which nonetheless puts you in hospital with urinary retention problems.

The first of these, the *Lycosa*, hunts its victims by jumping upto twenty centimetres in the air. In winter, it wraps its eggs in a cocoon. The second, the *Latrodectus*, spins a very sturdy web and unhurriedly awaits its prey. You see the prey caught in its toils, swaying in the wind.

Apart from the *Lycosa* and the *Latrodectus* there are no spiders in Apulia, except in the minds of those stung and possessed by them. Nor could the bite recur on the anniversary of its occurrence, since the tarantula is a purely imaginary animal.

What is the function of this non-existent spider? To produce happy trances. Once bitten, the women will be cured only by the *pizzica*, a dance accompanied by music and trances, a dance begun anew each year.

In June 1959, De Martino's team arrived at Galatina, a town with a 'well of Saint Paul' containing water allegedly beneficial to those bitten. And they tracked down a house where the rite took place.

Sacred images on the walls above a little altar. A big red cloth. No furniture. On the ground a white sheet and, on the sheet, the woman on her back. She's dressed in white with her hair down and a sash round her waist. A band, of musicians who cost an arm and a leg to hire, comprising a guitarist, an accordionist, a tambourine player and a violinist.

In honour of the mythic spider, the band plays the dance called the tarantella.

Merging herself with her tarantula, the woman writhes on her back like Élisabeth Blanchard on the altar steps at Loudun. But, unlike the possessed nun, she writhes rhythmically, her legs and head shaking in time with the music. Then she squats, stands, begins to hop, picks up a coloured handkerchief and stamps her feet fifty times every ten seconds. After rearing into the air she falls over backwards, inert, aided by the assistants who catch her in mid-air, wipe her brow and give her a drink of water. A perfect scenario.

The next morning, around ten, the woman cries out and her body arches, going into the famous hysterical 'crab' position, supported only on the tips of her toes and the back of her skull.

At lunchtime, she makes a number of barking cries. 'Release' comes at three in the afternoon; she sits up on a bed, smiles and remains still. To confirm her cure, the band launches into a tarantella of thanksgiving but she remains calm. Everyone falls to their knees.

Who delivers this release? It is Saint Paul himself, stung by Christ's spur when, as hostile non-believer, he was still called Saul of Tarsus. We may suspect he had many secrets to conceal.

With the exception of one man who has some primary schooling, the thirteen men and four women

studied by De Martino's team are illiterate. As agricul-
tural workers and the daughters or wives of smallholders,
these people live in houses without water or sanitation.
Like the Dakar women, they are, in 1959, poor people
leading particularly poverty-stricken lives. People of no
consequence. What a holiday the spider dance repre-
sents—with thanks to Saint Paul!

Since the ritual costs a great deal of money, these
destitute people plunge themselves into debt in order to
dance each year on the anniversary of first being bitten.
They remember it like a first kiss—the sun at its height
in the fields, then suddenly a burning puff of air; was it
a snake, a scorpion? They felt a bite and it was the tarantula. Though she was now a great age, one of them had
still kept the bundle of beanstalks in which the spider
had been hidden, a pious love-token.

Just one man had been stung by a *Latrodectus* and
hospitalized with a high fever, urinary retention and red
blotches on his skin. But when the medical episode was
over, he had asked for 'the sounds'. Though his body was
cured by a genuine pricking of the skin—an injection—
he needed the rite to heal his mind.

On 29 June, following the feast of Saint Paul, the
team attended a thanksgiving in the chapel. There was
neither music, coloured hangings nor proper ritual, but
a chaos of convulsive attacks in which the cries of the
tarantati were to be heard—A-hee-ee! A 'yelping', says
Ernesto de Martino, an animal's cry—the only traditional leftover from a lost ritual. Not without some sadness, the team resigns itself to the thought that it is
witnessing the last throes of the rite and that Tarantism
is on the way out. This was true in part.

In part only. Today there are no more illiterates
in the South of Italy. Tarantism and the *pizzica* are

recognized as local markers of 'identity', as part of the cultural heritage enthusiastically claimed by the region of Apulia. The dance of the Apulian *tarantati* can be seen in concerts and cultural gatherings; these days, courses are provided in *pizzica*.

It's the same now with the dance of the mythic spiders as with the parades of Dogon initiates and the ceremonies in which the Huli of Papua New Guinea make themselves up as birds of paradise and sport their enormous wigs. Shorn of their secrets and desacralized, they have become a show for tourists—a strange way for them to survive. But just as neither the Dogon nor the Huli have entirely abandoned their rites, no one knows in what part of the Tarento region the *tarantati* are hidden away today.

In 1959, a little cantilena had been sung, nonetheless, in the disorderly chapel. Here are the words:

Oh my Saint Paul of the *tarante*,
Who stings the girls between the hips,
Oh my Saint Paul of the scorpions,
Who stings the boys in the pants.

Pants? The text has *balloni*. You translate with decency when you're a scholar, but we get the message that the tarantula bites the vulva and the balls. The spider wants sex. Hence the trance and the dance.

The team reflected on all this and rummaged through the documents.

There was no lack of archive material. It revealed what was a very violent ritual over the course of history, each of the afflicted being armed with two swords which, at times, are deliberately driven into the flesh during the trance. There were blows on hands, feet and buttocks. There were wounds, blood and medical assistance. There were sometimes, fixed to the ceiling, ropes from which the *tarantati* swung. There were also pots of fragrant herbs—of basil, lemon verbena, mint and rue. A basin of water, vine branches. And coloured ribbons, for each tarantula chose its own colour.

Apulia was, in the past, a part of Magna Graecia, an immense territory peopled by Greek emigrant settlers which comprised part of Sicily, a little corner of Libya, a belt of land around Marseilles and another running along the Black Sea and the coasts of present-day Turkey, together with the entire 'boot' of what is now Italy. It would be in the mythic repertoire of ancient Greece that the team would find some of its explanations.

They were all fearsome.

A first hypothesis, relating to loving daughters. The festival of Aiora celebrates the memory of Erigone, the daughter of Icarus, who hanged herself after seeing her father's corpse. Following Erigone, an epidemic of suicides ravaged the virgins of Attica. To put an end to it, the oracle of Apollo made known the divine command that dolls should be hung from the branches of trees immediately after the appearance of the first buds of spring was celebrated. In this way the anger of the Sun was appeased, the anger of the god Apollo who was furious that Icarus, a mere mortal, had tried to rise as high as the god himself by flying.

A second hypothesis, relating to educated maidens. Arachne, after whom the arachnid genus is named, was a young weaver who dared to challenge Athena in a weaving contest. A bad idea. Athena struck the girl on the forehead with a shuttle and Arachne ran off to hang herself. Taking pity on her, the goddess turned her into a spider but forced her to live hanging from a web.

Underlying the flying webs of the *Latrodectus* are these hanging dolls and this girl turned spider; the tarantula victims swing from their ropes like hanged girls.

A third hypothesis, relating to girls with a sweetheart. Lyssa, the goddess of mad rage in animals, is the granddaughter of Ouranos, sprung from the blood of his severed penis. She imparts madness. She is the sting of the gadfly. It is she who goads the unfortunate Io, beloved of Zeus and pursued by his wife Hera who forces her to flee to the ends of the Earth. Zeus transforms Io into a cow and Lyssa becomes a gadfly. The poor girl/cow owes her name to her cry of Io, Io—not far removed from the 'A-hee-ee' of the women stung by spiders. Io will find rest in Egypt, land of groves and calm waters.

Now, the archives show that most of the time the *tarantati* went dancing *ad aquas, ad fontes, ad ramum viridem*—that is to say, towards water, springs and green boughs. In 1959, only a single well remained.

A last hypothesis, relating to married women. In Apulia there were cults of Dionysus, god of trance and intoxication and a fanatical lover of Italy. 'Thou who watchest over famed Italia,' says a chorus in *Antigone*. At Taranto (Tarentum), the city sacred to Dionysus where the Bacchantes celebrated his cult, an incredible episode occurred in the second century BCE, beginning in Apulia and ending in Rome.

CHAPTER 10

The Bellower
(The Loire)

Why was Rome the site of the terrible doings of the Bacchantes, as told by the historian Livy?

Thirty thousand inhabitants of Tarentum had been reduced to slavery in that city, bringing with them their family cults the same way the black slaves took voodoo with them from the Gulf of Guinea to Brazil and the Caribbean.

In 186 BCE, the city of Rome—*the* City—makes the apparent discovery that the Bacchanalia, which happen at night, in reality provide a cover for rapes, murders and orgies. False testimony, false accusations and all the machinery of witch persecution are unleashed against the Bacchanalian trances. Where does this fury against a Greek sect come from?

From Roman morality: women weren't allowed to drink wine, a drink thought to induce abortion. From a political threat: the Bacchantes are the only sectarian group to contain participants from all classes and not to discriminate socially—even against slaves. Lastly, from the eternal danger of southern Italy, the crucible of rioting and insurrection.

Rome makes its decision and the cult of Dionysus will subsequently require strict authorization from the *Praetor urbanus* and the Senate (with a quorum, for the purpose, of a hundred senators). It is suspected of having seven thousand initiates. Those flouting the regulations risk the death penalty. The Bacchanalia become a site of resistance.

Two years later, after large numbers of the Bacchantes of Rome have taken refuge in the town of Tarentum, a rebellion erupts and is difficult to quell. Rebellion breaks out again in 182 BCE and the next year the Senate orders stern measures to prevent the 'scourge' from spreading. The Bacchanalia will be subject to repression for more than a century.

In 1959, the *tarantati* observed by De Martino's team are suffering from symptoms almost two thousand years old, symptoms of the same rebellion of the poor against the North. Dionysus, now concealed behind the figure of Saint Paul, went on rendering women 'beside themselves', far from their homes, their feet leaping and hopping, as light as spiders.

Dionysus, the god of equality and of liberty for women, was worshipped in the form of a mask with wide, staring eyes. Eyes staring forward. Hypnotically.

He presents himself always as a foreigner, coming from India, which he has conquered, returning to his home at Thebes in Greece.

He is a travelling god. Born of the union of a mortal woman and Zeus, the god-child is hunted by his father's wife, the eternally jealous goddess Hera. From her comes his madness and, like Io, he wanders, before ultimately being rescued by his grandmother Rhea who binds her grandson's madness in a robe, the first costume of the Bacchanalia, and crowns him with fresh vine leaves.

By his mere presence he brings the married women out of their houses, incites them to desert the conjugal home and dance away the night in the woods where they tear heifers limb from limb with their bare hands. When he doesn't receive a warm welcome, he chastises.

At Thebes, the king wants to expel him. These foreigners always bring disorder . . . Go on, out with you! He's got to go! But the god won't be driven out and takes reprisals. The king's head will be separated from his body by the very hands of his old mother after she, in a trance, mistakes him for a lion. As one of the Bacchantes, she has superhuman strength.

Athens receives the god badly. The Athenian males are immediately afflicted with priapism and are incapable of losing their erections. Punishments for the men and trances for the women, some of whom the god occasionally chastises.

The Namnetes were Bacchantes who lived on an island opposite the present-day city of Nantes at the mouth of the Loire. They lived without men in a life of total devotion to Dionysus.

Once a year, the god would suddenly require them to change the roof of his sanctuary, the whole of the work having to be performed between sunrise and sunset on a single day—just as Dionysus made wine from the vine in one day.

That day, the Bacchantes of Nantes set to work, each carrying her burden. Every year without fail, one of these women would drop her plank, stumble and fall. And unfailingly the other women would fling themselves on the fallen one and tear her to pieces, brandishing her limbs as they circled the sanctuary uttering the cry of Dionysus: Ev-o-hé—Ah-hee-ee.

Springing far from home. The trance of Dionysus begins with the foot. The Bacchant leaps out of her seat and 'quick-footed, looses her leg'. The Greek name for the Dionysian trance, *ekpedan*, means 'leap out', 'leap away'.

A conjugal eclipse. Aristoxenus, the Greek musicologist of Tarentum, left behind a precise description of the trances of the Dionysian women between Locri and Reggio at the toe-end of the Italian boot. All of them came out leaping and ran 'away'—towards water and the countryside.

The remedy—song and music. In the same place.

But under orders from the god the trance continues, this time in hopping mode. With little leaps, like the jumping *Lycosa*. It was normal that a woman with a load in her arms, on a manless island lying off the coast opposite Nantes, should stumble. 'The history of the Dionysus of the island relates the violence of a god who might, throughout the year, seem to be another, but who, for one single day, is entirely himself, reminding the forgetful that he is, in all exactitude, the inner Foreigner, the god who puts all to fire and the sword as the fancy takes him,' writes Marcel Detienne in *Dionysos à ciel ouvert* (1986; *Dionysos at Large*, 1989).

Driving away foreigners is an ill-omened thing; the inner Foreigner will not be treated that way.

The god has a nickname: Bromios, the bellower. And he loves noise, an old childhood memory. When he was small and threatened by the Titans, Dionysus was hidden by the armour-clad, helmeted Corybantes who danced noisily, striking their metal shields to the sound of a little drum. They worshipped a goddess from a distant land, the great Cybele from Phrygia, an area in the West of present-day Turkey. And if they made noise, they did so to conceal the crying of the son of Zeus who mustn't be discovered. The noise and the sound of clashing weapons plunged the Corybantes into a trance so violent that they required medical attention.

The nurses, known as the 'healers of the sickness of the Corybantes', took charge of them. They tended to the bodies in their trance states and brought them back to the dance which regulated their palpitating hearts. These were the assistants—and perhaps the first such.

It is this leaping god whose mask is said to have presided over the first theatrical performances—on the stage stands a pole and on that pole is a hypnotic face with pointed ears and wide, staring eyes directed straight at the audience. Did he preside over the human sacrifices which some imagine to have occurred on the tragic stage? He would be capable of it. The dawn of Greek theatre arose beneath the dark sun of Dionysian trances.

Two millennia later, theatre in Europe revisited the trance state, disseminating excitement, disgust or joy. In 1969, the South African actor Roy Hart, after working extensively on the voice—in, among other places, a psychiatric hospital—presented a performance on the Bacchantes at the Nancy International Festival. The members of the Roy Hart Theatre drew on all the potential of the human cry.

Hart's teacher Alfred Wolfsohn had discovered the range of human voices in the trenches of the Great War, listening to the howling of the soldiers. It was dread that underlay these terrifying cries. Between psychotherapy and sacred theatre, the theatrical sessions of the Roy Hart Theatre gripped audiences through the fusion of a group unified by shouts of joy, stupor, terror and ecstasy. Trance was not far away.

But not quite there either.

Joy Sorman describes Joey Starr as very much akin to a shaman: 'Joey Starr ready to pounce. With his naked, lean torso—stiff, muscular, veiny and taut as a drum skin. Pectorals, abdominals, his stomach double-glazed, resembling a bullet-proof vest. Impenetrable. Joey a force of nature, a force of 'highs' and sound. How nature, 'highs' and sound—these elements together—form a body, forge a body, produce it, inside and out. What we call a personal history, the course of a life. Where you start out from.'

The artiste's stage name comes from that of the American plantation slave—Joey, the house negro. Didier Morville, alias Joey Starr, abused in childhood by a cruel father and with several convictions for assault and battery, particularly on women. Into eclipse in prison on a regular basis. Dangerous. Leaping, drum skin, force of nature, forged body, uninitiated shaman.

CHAPTER 11

Madonna Oriente and the Animal of Ecstasy

In the Ariège region in 1280 she is called Bensozia, at Trier in 1310 she is called Diana while the woman Sibillia, speaking before a Dominican inquisitor in Lombardy in 1384, calls her Good Mistress Richella and Madonna Oriente.

Every Thursday night, Sibillia visited Oriente and her company. She lowered her head and said, 'Be well, Madona Horiente' and Madonna Oriente replied, 'Welcome, my daughters.' Apart from asses—'because they had carried the cross'—all the animals were there.

Madonna Oriente foretold the future and taught the use of herbs to treat illnesses, how to recover stolen objects and how to break evil spells. If Christ is the master of the world, Madonna Oriente is the mistress of society, capable of resuscitating animals provided that, after eating their flesh, their bones are tied up in a bag of skin. Madonna Oriente strikes the bag with the pommel of her stick and the cattle revive within the hour. This is the Good Mistress (*bona domina*).

Before the early fifteenth century, few consequences ensued from paying her a visit. In 1457, Bishop Nicolas of Cusa treated the old women's stories as folly and imaginings, merely condemning them to public penitence and a short spell in prison. The stake? No, that would strengthen Satan's image.

It wasn't yet the era of sabbaths which would also be the age of witches burnt at the stake. The Black Death, which had arrived from the steppes of central Asia, the land of shamanism, was beginning to ravage a Europe that would soon find people to blame for it.

Up until the fifteenth century in Scotland, France, the Rhineland, Friuli and Sicily, women spoke in all innocence of being swept away in ecstasies in the night, mounted on animals that carried them rapidly over great distances, in obedience to the orders of the mistress of Oriente's society.

Madonna Oriente isn't like Dionysus; she wages benign wars to protect the corn or the vines. The Italian historian Carlo Ginzburg has described the rites of the Benandanti of Friuli, nightriders who went off in a trance armed with plant stalks to fight the Malandanti, the forces of Evil, destroyers of the harvests. Apart from Madonna Oriente's group, there's a great deal of riding in the trance state. The Wilde Jagd or Wild Hunt, the Mesnie furieuse (Furious Household), the Mesnie Helle-quin (Household of Hellequin), the chasse Arthur (Arthur's Hunt) are so many fantastical armies of the night, spread over the entire European continent: France, Spain, Italy, Germany, Britain and Scandinavia. In all these night rides the dead appear—in a procession or as a troop—particularly during the twelve days that separate Christmas from the festival of Epiphany.

Just as Dionysus was long perpetuated in Apulia in the guise of Saint Paul, other festivals lie hidden beneath the Christian ones. On the nights between 24 December and 6 January in the Celtic calendar, in the Teutonic world and in ancient Rome, the dead walked abroad. It was their moment. From the rites aimed at celebrating the wandering dead while neutralizing the dangers they posed, some enduring fragments have come down to us as ways of protecting ourselves from the—fearsome—souls of dead children.

Before our very eyes we have the processions of children in fancy dress, harassing householders for sweets at Halloween. And then, as Lévi-Strauss showed us in 'Father Christmas Executed', we also have the fine figure of Father Christmas, distant heir of the King of Saturnalia, the old fellow who does all he can to soothe the souls of dead children and send them back into the afterlife. Take your presents and off with you! Away with them!

Father Christmas is a pagan. That's why on 24 December 1951, the clergy of Dijon Cathedral decided to burn the dreadful heretic, his effigy being sent up in smoke before the eyes of the pupils of the Catholic (private) schools.

The deputy mayor of Dijon at the time was Canon Kir, a former Resistance fighter and a member of the Centre National des Indépendants (CNI), a political grouping on the Right of the Right. However, on 25 December, on Dijon's town-hall roof, a floodlit Father Christmas came back to life before an audience of state-school children. Executing Father Christmas wasn't a popular act.

Canon Kir came from Alsace, a land of witchcraft. No doubt he had a pretty good understanding of the shamanic past of a figure that originated in ancient Rome, a prince of freedom dressed in red and white who clambers over the roofs of our houses today and does promotions in department stores.

For Ginzburg there could be no doubt. There was in Europe a Celtic substratum, based, from Brittany to Friuli, on 'a popular religion of the dead'.

That substratum reaches as far as Sicily, to which island the Breton knights who landed with the Normans were able to spread their Celtic legends. And so we see King Arthur shown astride the back of a great goat on the ornate tiled floor of the Cathedral of Otranto and said to slumber in a cave beneath Mount Etna. And we see Perceval and Lancelot journeying to the Land of the Dead, to castles separated from the world by a bridge, a heath or a sea. As for Morgan Le Fay, she is overlaid on two Celtic goddesses—the Irish Morrigan and the Welsh Modron, both of them 'good mistresses' also, rulers over the afterlife.

There are sixteenth-century documents originating in Sicily in which the image of Madonna Oriente, not previously depicted with animal characteristics, changes significantly. In Sicily, when brought before the inquisitors, women and girls say that they fly away at night to engage in revels with the 'women from outside' (*donni di fuori*) who have cats' paws or equine hooves. These companies of women have at their centre a Matron, also known as the Teacher, the Greek Mistress, the Wise Sibilla or the Queen of the Fairies.

Here the animals make their appearance.

The town of Troina in Sicily was called Engyon when Plutarch wrote of it. Engyon was the site of the very famous cult of the Mothers, goddesses who induced ecstasy in their followers, followed by frenzied trances. Now, who were they?

They were bears. The mothers are the good, nurturing bears who, when they were nymphs, raised the young Zeus whose mother wanted to hide him from his cannibalistic father Kronos, God of Time. When he had become king of the gods, Zeus transformed his nurturing nymphs into the constellations of the Great and Little Bear (Ursa Major and Ursa Minor).

Tracking the bear, Ginzburg reminds us that Diana/Artemis, virgin and huntress, the mistress of the animals, was venerated as a nurse and as protector of pregnancies and virgins. At Brauron (Vravron), one of her sanctuaries, the goddess was attended by girls known as 'bears'. And in Crete there is a Cave of the Bear where images of Diana/Artemis and her brother Apollo have been found. A Virgin of the Bear's Cave (*Panaghia arkoudiotissa*) is worshipped there today, the mother of Christ being said to have turned to stone a bear she had disturbed.

Nicolas of Cusa told how women caressed by the Good Mistress Richella had felt a hairy hand pass over their cheeks. Did Jeanne des Anges know that the name of the patron saint of her religious order derived from the she-bear?

Ursula, the ursine saint. The Ursulines were secretly cut out to be heirs to the furry-pawed she-bears.

The moment has come to seek out the furs.

The first person to make the connection between the trances of the Arctic Circle shamans and those of Diana's faithful followers was the sinister judge Pierre de Lancre, the great witch-hunter of early-seventeenth-century Béarn. He calls these strange characters from Lapland 'magi' and it has to be recognized, he says, that though they once lived in the northern lands, in Ireland and the Baltic countries, they have since spread all over Europe.

So we had shamans and we didn't know it.

De Lancre also adds werewolves. An eighty-year-old named Thiess confessed to his judges that he was a werewolf. The trial took place in 1692 at Jürgensburg—Jaunpils in present-day Latvia. Old Thiess stated that, as a werewolf armed with steel whips, he hunted the devil and his witches. Witches stole seed corn and for that reason they had to be fought and defeated, he said.

The judges tried to make the old man confess that he had struck a pact with the Devil. He wouldn't yield on this, however, repeating that he was sure he was going to Heaven. Disconcerted by this figure of a good werewolf as protector of the harvests, the judges sentenced him to ten lashes.

Old Thiess was lucky. Since the fifteenth century, the period in which the myth of the witches' Sabbath crystallized, the werewolf had been seen as an evil creature that devoured children and animals.

Where does one become a werewolf? Among the Neuri mentioned by Herodotus, a mysterious people doubtless of Baltic origin. But also in Ireland, in the Germanic countries and throughout the Baltic lands.

How does one become a werewolf? More or less the same way as one acts the reindeer in Siberia. The individual falls into a deep, ecstatic sleep; then, in his wolf form, he undresses, hangs his clothes on the branches of a tree or lays them on the ground, urinates all around, then crosses the river. His wolf's soul journeys among the dead.

No women.

An enormous werewolf figures in Stephenie Meyer's *Twilight* saga. He is a Native American of the Quileute tribe, whose reservation is at La Push in Washington state, a place of pilgrimage today for the fans of *Twilight*, the so-called 'twilighters'. The fiercely protective werewolf pal is always by the heroine's side whereas his function ought really be to kill vampires. In a show of noble sentiment, an animalistic *coup de foudre* sees the Native American werewolf fall in love with the half-vampire, half-human girl.

Wolves are not the only trance animals. In Hungary the *táltos*, transformed by trances into horses or bulls, are at pains not to be mistaken for witches whom they fight. God in person forms them in this way in the bellies of their mothers to make them fighters in Heaven's cause.

They are small, taciturn and great milk-drinkers, these being the signs by which they can be recognized. Their initiation begins with three days of an ecstatic, dream-filled sleep. Then the initiate, suffused with a sudden warmth, stammers out some incoherent words and is transformed. He then flies off for the battle which, if the *táltos* win, will ensure good harvests. In the morning, like all shamans, he wakes up groaning and in pain.

The same battles of ecstatic sleepers whose spirits take to the air are seen in the Balkans, Slovenia, Dalmatia and Montenegro, as well as in Lapland, among the Ossetians in the Caucasus, in Circassia, Rumania and even in Corsica in the Sartenais region and the Niolo mountains, where, rather than fight evil spirits, the *mazzeri* pursue nocturnal vendettas among themselves.

The map of shamanic animal transformations drawn up by Ginzburg doesn't cover whole continents. It's a patchwork and isn't the same as the map of Madonna Oriente, the *bona domina*, who drew all the animals towards her, except the asses. There is one map for women and another for men.

Madonna Oriente is the mistress of the animals, and the trance state sees women become keepers of the herds or packs. But in the case of the werewolf, the stallion and the bull, it's men who turn into animals in the trance state.

Unsurprisingly, like their counterparts on the American continent, they use mushrooms.

The first of these is the *claviceps purpurea* fungus or rye ergot, responsible for very serious epidemics known as ergotism or Saint Anthony's Fire which produce gangrenous or convulsive symptoms, violent cramps and loss of consciousness. As is well known, rye ergot contains an alkaloid that was synthesized in 1943 as Lysergic Acid Diethylemide or LSD, the drug that sent people on long 'acid trips'.

But the *claviceps purpurea* fungus was also one of the traditional medicines used to induce abortion, to stop haemorrhages, even to ease contractions in difficult births.

Under the influence of rye ergot we see the whole of the shamanic cycle in action: convulsions, shaking, violent collapse, inert sleep and visions.

Visions!

When the shaman rises from the apparently dead state into which he is plunged by his amours with a daughter of the forest, he tells of what he has seen, since this is his function. Visions are one of the ways out of the trance. A vision is something that has to be put into words; you impart it to others, use words, become socialized once again. This is what Jeanne des Anges did to shake off her demons. To speak of your visions, dreams and phantasies is to prepare yourself to be healed.

The second trance fungus is the *amanita muscaria*, the handsome toadstool with the bright red, white-speckled round cap found in fairy tales. Though not lethal, the *amanita muscaria* contains ibotenic acid, a powerful sleep-inducing agent, and muscimol, which causes hallucinations. Known commonly as the fly algaric, the *amanita muscaria* grows beneath birches and fir trees in Europe and Siberia.

It's found in the woods and forests of the areas where the great witch trials took place—in the Alps, the Pyrenees and the Loire region. A banal forest fungus causes lethargic sleep and hallucinations. Should we see a link between the *amanita muscaria* and demonic possession?

Ginzburg raises the question and describes a European case from the fourteenth century. During a heresy trial in Piedmont, Bilia la Castagna was accused of having distributed a drink based on toad excrement. The inquisitors took a very serious view and she was burnt at the stake.

And how are these fungi known everywhere? As *pisse de chien* (dog piss), *vesse-de-loup* (wolf fart). As fox droppings or puma droppings.

This is not all. The *amanita muscaria* is often given toad-related names: in Britain, the toadstool; in France, the *crapaudin* or *pain de crapaud*; in China, the toad fungus. The toad being a fairy animal, a magical creature, it can transform itself into a prince charming or a string of pearls.

Everyone knew this except the inquisitors, who were determined to eradicate by fire all trace of the popular religion of the dead, the merest hint of shamanism, and anything redolent in any way whatever of the myths and rites of the pagans. Zero tolerance for paws, fur, snouts and hairy hands.

They were unsuccessful. In the fantasy fiction genre, new animal metamorphoses are invented each year. In Philip Pullman's fantastical *His Dark Materials* saga, published between 1995 and 2000, the characters each possess a 'daemon', an animal endowed with speech, to whom they are connected by an invisible umbilical cord.

When this is cut, a state of psychical inertia ensues—no one can live, feel, love or think without his or her 'daemon'. Where adolescents are concerned, there's a special aspect to this—since they are not yet fully formed, their 'daemon' may change species as their emotions change. Just as Socrates had his shamanic *daimon*, which warned him by discreet trances that an event was going to change his life, so the children of *His Dark Materials* are warned of dangers by the animals they have at their sides.

It will come as no surprise to see them finding a rescuer in the Arctic wastes in the form of a bear clad in armour.

In the immense shamanic substructure that runs from Asia to Ireland, no trace is to be found of the ecstatic transformation of humans into spiders or bats. Yet Hollywood has achieved this. As new incarnations of the good werewolf—protectors now not of the harvests but of cities—Batman and Spiderman are marvellous innovations of American cinema. By contrast, as a reformed burglar, Catwoman is more of a throwback to the old model of the 'women from outside' with their cat-like paws.

CHAPTER 12

Trans

The trance goes animal. Or passes from one sex to the other. It switches species or changes gender.

There are countless examples of witches speaking with men's voices, like Mälkam Ayyähou the old healer observed by Leiris in northern Ethiopia. In trances, men find their female voices.

In his home between Chennai and Madurai in southern India, I met a man who, in a state of trance, was a woman. Nothing about his appearance was feminine. He had a little moustache, a pot belly, a white loin-cloth and a deep voice. He was married with four children in an exemplary Indian family—well-turned-out children, a self-effacing wife.

His followers call him Our Mother, for his sex is of little importance. Having been visited by a cobra in his cradle, this son of Catholics understood at the age of twelve that he was a Shakti, an incarnation of female power, endowed with an ability to foretell the future. So the oracles began, twice a week, attracting immense crowds to whom Our Mother prescribed the wearing of a universal red, because all humans have the same red blood.

So it was in a red loincloth that he came out for the ceremony, supported by female assistants in red saris. Moving between two lines of woman shaking sistrums, he raised himself up on tiptoe, trembled and fell, to be caught in welcoming arms. Such a rapid eclipse. Not even two seconds and here he is as Mother.

Seated on a bed of sea-buckthorn leaves, that sacred tree with its therapeutic properties, Our Mother spoke in a woman's voice. When she comes out of her trance, she returns to her man's body, but for the rest of the time 'he' is Our Mother. And, in this latter persona, She has built a temple, a university, a hospital and numerous hotels.

In India this surprises no one. Of the three major gods in the Hindu pantheon, one, Shiva, at times assumes a form combining his male and female representations. Ardhanarishwara, a bisexual version of Shiva, is a woman on the left side, from the jewels on her head to those on her toes, and a man on the right side, with a flat torso and muscular thighs.

There's no castration here, no surgery, nothing. The trance alone transforms this fine father into a Mother and prophetess.

Nor is there any surgery on the islands of Samoa for the Fa'afafine.

The Samoan model of virility finds its highest embodiment through the game of rugby. Its players are paragons of physical strength in an Oceania where, for many countries, the national rugby team is an economic resource and a subject of pride.

Now it is here in a rugby region that the Fa'afafine are found: literally, *fa'a*—like—and *fafine*—women.

The Fa'afafine are 'men as women' who, from childhood, dress up as girls, care for the children of the family, perform women's tasks and live in feminine space which, but for the odd exception, doesn't overlap with that of rugby. In their love lives the Fa'afafine need men, as partners in sex and affection. But the Fa'afafine don't allow anyone to call them homosexual men.

The Fa'afafine are quite simply women. They're in no way entangled in their birth bodies and not calling for any change of gender, since they're a clearly defined gender: man as woman. They are not in any way disturbed. The Pacific Ocean seems to have little trouble accommodating the third gender so ardently sought after in other worlds.

Inuit societies, which are fearfully complex, include a 'third social sex', described at some length by the ethnologist Bernard Saladin d'Anglure.

Act 1: The newborn are given the name and identity of their dead grandparents, who dominate their parents symbolically until they themselves become parents. These names have no gender.

Act 2: Names can therefore pass from one sex to the other, in two-thirds of instances from boys to girls. But, in that case, the children will be brought up clothed as the other sex and required to learn its tasks: 'inverted socialization', as Saladin d'Anglure terms it.

In 1971, when he arrived on the island of Igloolik in Baffin Bay, Saladin d'Anglure began to have conversations with a woman named Iqallijuq. She related her pre-birth memories from when she was the soul of her maternal grandfather, Savviuqtalik, whose identity she necessarily assumed.

And here, through the voice of his granddaughter, the ancestor Savviuqtalik begins to relate his memories as a foetus.

He was dead, he was cold, and he knew he was going to be reincarnated in the womb of his own daughter, into which he slipped while she was urinating. It's a very small igloo and he's very cramped there, until the day he can't stay there any longer and it's time to come out.

I couldn't get to the entrance. To its left were some male implements. I reached out and grasped them, but at that point I had a premonition that my father was going to drown as he was hunting on the ice-floe. The one who bore my name (my eponym), Savviuqtalik, had expressed the desire before he died that he should return as a woman, as he was weary of the excessive cold, exertion and risks associated with hunting. Suddenly aware that I could be very cold and die like my father if I used these tools, I put them back and took hold of the female utensils, an oil lamp and a little knife. Then I closed my eyes and, with great effort, came out of the igloo. But as I came out, my penis retracted, my perineum split into a vulva and, from having previously been male, I became a female, a *sipiniq*' [a 'transsexual', says Saladin d'Anglure].

In this way the child Iqallijuq is born, a grandfather reincarnated in his granddaughter. He/she wears male clothing, drives sleds, looks after the dogs and goes hunting. She/he thinks of her/himself as a boy, thus contradicting the grandfather's wish to be born a girl, but contenting her mother, who sees in her her dearly beloved father.

As soon as Iqallijuq first menstruates, her mother makes her a female coat and women's trousers to go with it. Furious at the idea of becoming a girl again, Iqallijuq tears it to pieces. It took her some time to become a woman, but the benefits of her male upbringing weren't lost on her and she was a good hunter and a good mother, a man and a woman at the same time.

For, at puberty, everyone returns to their biological sex.

Act 3: Going back to other clothing and other postures, changing social sex and behaving as a girl when
one has lived as a boy brings on profound crises. Those
concerned will be shamans, 'moving astride boundaries';
they will be mediators between the natural and supernatural worlds since, given their crossing of boundaries,
they have access to Qaumaniq—light.

But Inuit children are given several names that may
be of different sexes. So what effect does this have? At
times they display the attributes of both sexes simultaneously, at others they choose between the two, as circumstances dictate. They are one or the other, or both
at once—an end to the difference between two sexes.
The shamans' trances draw on this source, where the
waters of the three genders mingle.

In Siberian shamanism, it so happens that some
shamans, being united with supernatural husbands, dress
as women for the sessions, foregoing the headdress with
the iron deer-antlers and adopting 'feminine ways'. In
life, they are married and are fathers and heads of families; everyone understands the ritual cross-dressing, as is
the case with 'Our Mother', the South Indian Tamil. But
it also happens that a shaman, changed into a woman to
please her spirit-husband, marries a man. Clandestinely,
the shaman/married-woman has a mistress and children.

The fate of the shamanesses of Siberia is very different. In principle, strict equality prevails, with men and
women both having a calling to shamanize. But this is
not actually the case. With the handicap of menstrual
blood, the shamaness cannot overcome her nature as
woman. She'll never be the son-in-law of a supernatural
father-in-law and, in the mythic hunt, she'll not be able
to fulfil the role of hunter completely. When, by ill luck,
a woman is seduced by an animal male spirit, she'll go
off into the forest, lose her reason and die there.

The usual role of women in Siberia is to assist the shaman husband, helping him put on his costume, holding the accessories, providing the accompaniment to his voice. And yet it's the shamanesses who have the place of honour in the yourts.

The explanation lies in myth. A great many changes of gender are to be seen in the 'sister epics', admirable texts.

Such as the following.

Fearsome the Clever, aged fifteen and his little sister Fairest One, who are orphans, live alone. Overcome by a yearning for game, Fearsome goes out hunting and is killed by an old woman who cuts him in two. The boy's horse returns home, carrying its master's coat over the saddle. The sister realizes what has happened and faints—a solid sign of an eclipse. When she comes to, the horse tells her that only Wayward-Betrothed, the king's daughter, can revive her brother. With sadness, Fairest One cuts her hair, puts on her brother's coat and sets off to find the pre-destined fiancée. Off she goes as a young man.

On the way she comes across the old woman, kills and burns her and, weeping, gathers up the bones—all the bones—of her dead brother, which she hides in a cave. Surmounting various obstacles with the aid of animal allies—an ant, a frog, a bird of prey—she arrives at the encampment where the king has organized games to celebrate the wedding of his only daughter, Wayward-Betrothed. But she has no brother with whom an exchange of fiancées can be made in customary form. To win the fiancée of her dead brother, a now unrecognizable Fairest One presents herself as a candidate in the games.

After innumerable ordeals, the king is forced to give his daughter's hand in marriage to the sister disguised as her own brother. Since a dwarf shamaness is the only one to see that the fiancé is a woman in disguise, the king shuts away his daughter with his future son-in-law to have them 'play-act' lovemaking. We shall see what we shall see.

The first dangerous night. Steadfastly, Fairest One turns her back and falls asleep; but, on the right thigh of her intended, Wayward-Betrothed has seen a crescent-shaped sign she was looking out for. She is now firmly convinced. The suitor is a man. The next day the marriage is concluded. And the couple leave in great haste. No time for a wedding night.

On the way back, Fairest One leaves her wife just long enough to go and fetch the bones from the cave. She lays them out on the bed, re-forming the skeleton and dresses it in her clothes which she leaves behind. She disappears.

When Wayward-Betrothed tries to wake her, she finds the skeleton in her place and is furious. The horse intervenes and issues instructions. The young bride sits astride the skeleton three times and it is once again covered with flesh. Then she cracks her whip three times and the body comes alive. A happy ending.

And Fairest One? She runs off stark naked into the forest where she turns into a fine, plump reindeer. Three years later, upon her return, her resuscitated brother marries his sister out of the family to a man of athletic build. Thus is patriarchy restored and, for the sister, the eclipse is at an end.

Ever brave and devoted, the sisters are the ones who find the fiancée so that they may then receive their husbands from the hands of the brother they have saved.

They assist. And always, with sadness, they cut their hair before transforming themselves into their dismembered brothers. But that doesn't last.

Once the fiancée has been married off, the sisters will fall back under the yoke of their husbands, returning to woman's estate. This is their limit, the same limit as that of the shamanesses. They are heroic and honoured, but secondary.

Elsewhere, surgery plays its part as it has always done. In India, the hijra, who are sometimes intersexual at birth, are most often castrated in adolescence at their own request. They form a tight-knit group which is now supported by defence associations, since their financial resources are being depleted by the enrichment of the middle classes who are less responsive to magical traditions.

There's a mythic reference behind the hijra—from the Mahabharata epic. After gambling away his kingdom, wealth, wife and four brothers, the head of the Pandava clan was forced to spend twelve years in the wilderness. In the thirteenth year, all the members of the family would be required to 'find positions for themselves' without revealing their identities.

Arjuna, the handsomest of the brothers and the most skilled archer, found himself a place as a eunuch in a king's harem. Dressed in a sari, perfumed and bejewelled, Arjuna would be dancing master to the queen and her women. At the end of the ordeal, with his exile terminated, Arjuna became a warrior once more, as indeed he had never ceased to be beneath his sari.

Are these hijra shamanic? Of course they are. And they certainly inspire fear: I've seen my Indian women friends, who can tell them a long way off, step aside muttering, though they also bring out their purses just in case. The hijra are feared, for their man/woman status affords them magic powers. When they arrive at a family gathering, there's a rush to meet their needs for fear of the evil eye. As for sorcery, they can cast spells; they also know how to give blessings.

If anyone recoils even slightly from them, you see them react, quick to curse when they sense contempt. When they dance, magnificently, in the style of the Gypsies of India, the hijra are almost in a trance, but this is in a country where trance states are within everyone's reach. Their cross-dressing is, at times, a masterpiece, but the ones you see prostituting themselves at the motorway tollbooths give vent, beneath their saris and sparkling jewellery, to their male side, yelling at the top of their men's voices at the lorry drivers in a country that still prosecutes homosexuality, though the Supreme Court of the Indian Union recently opened the door to official recognition.[3]

In many countries today, contemporary surgery knows how to reassign sexes. For a girl who wants to be a boy, there can be mammoplasty and a penis graft. For a lad who wants to be a lass, breasts can be inflated hormonally, the Adam's apple and the genitals can be surgically removed, followed by vaginoplasty. In both cases there can be operations, anaesthesia, post-operative care, work on the voice, cosmetic surgery for the face. Painlessly?

The sex-reassignment route involves physical and mental pain not unlike a long initiation, since an initiation consists in completing a human being who was born unfinished. The child was perhaps born intersexual, perhaps forced surgically by its parents—or perhaps merely psychically—into a gender that was not its own: it was not complete.

3 The Supreme Court of India, since December 2013, has reinstated its ban on homosexuality.—Ed.

For a long time, the first pain in the transition state came from psychologists, psychiatrists and psychoanalysts who saw the desire to 'change sex' as part of a pathology. Since 2010 in France, however, this no longer applies. 'Transexuals'—they don't like that name—are no longer regarded as mentally ill.

Once transformed, the 'child' will move into 'adulthood' with his new gender. He or she will be an 'ex-transsexual' or an 'ex-transexual'. Shamanic? Perhaps. The eclipse was so long.

At the other end of the 'third sex' spectrum, the most mythic 'trannies' are hermaphrodites, endowed with pneumatic breasts and penises. What in English are called 'she-males'. These don't exist, of course, and yet, look, they do. Those rounded breasts with that erect prick—the unimaginable body. A thousand sensual pleasures in prospect, a thousand *petites morts* to be enjoyed. One of the oldest fantasies in the world is in rude health and has its place in the Shangri-la of hard-core sex.

CHAPTER 13

DSM III@Sorcery.org
(USA; Canada)

In 1952, American psychiatrists published a classification handbook for all mental illnesses. In what has since come to be called *The Diagnostic and Statistical Manual of Mental Disorders*—more commonly, DSM—they counted sixty of them. At the time of the first DSM, the American classification was highly dependent on psychoanalytic classifications.

DSM II was published in 1968, listing one hundred and forty-five categories of mental disorder. In 1980, DSM III appeared, eliminating all the psychoanalytic categories and leaving only 'facts': two hundred and thirty categories of mental disorder. In 1994, DSM IV listed four hundred and ten.

DSM V is planned for 2013 and mention is made on the preparatory site of 'sexual and gender identity disorders'.

The 1980 manual, DSM III, included a novel category—multiple personalities. The disorder wasn't a new one. It was in 1906 that Henry Morton Prince, a doctor, published *The Dissociation of Personality* which analysed the case of Sally Beauchamp, the pseudonym of Clara Ellen Fowler, a student who, under hypnosis, turned out to be inhabited by three personalities: B I, B II and B III, including a saint and an impudent she-devil.

In 1954, in *The Journal of Abnormal and Social Psychology*, two therapists using hypnosis brought to light the case of Eve, a woman inhabited by several personalities. This gave rise to an award-winning book and film, *The Three Faces of Eve* (1957). As soon as these appeared, the therapists received many calls from depressed women complaining of the same symptoms.

The success created the syndrome.

Still in 1954, Dr Cornelia Wilbur, a psychiatrist who qualified at the University of Michigan, began the treatment of Shirley Ardell Mason who played host to sixteen different personalities and, after eleven years of therapy, integrated them all into her person. In 1973, from the pen of Flora Rheta Schreiber, a science journalist, came a biographical novel entitled *Sybil*, relating the treatment of the above-mentioned Shirley whose identity was concealed beneath this name. It was an enormous, worldwide success and was made into a TV film.

The same year saw the release of *The Exorcist*, a horror film directed by William Friedkin in which the entire repertoire of demonic possession was manifested simultaneously in one little girl.

In the opening scenes an exorcist priest discovered the statue of a demon. And where should he find it but in Iraq.

The DSM III classification of 1980 came out of the prodigious effect produced by the publication of *Sybil*: cases of multiple personality grew too numerous to count and were shown on American talk shows by TV presenters addressing themselves directly to the 'alternating' personalities, the various 'guests' harboured by the patients. The Christian therapists' and counsellors' lobby also joined in and a day came when the syndrome was accepted as a legal classification.

In 1975, Billy Milligan, a criminal with previous offences to his name, was accused of three rapes that he could not recall having committed. He was examined by a first psychiatrist who concluded that he was schizophrenic, an old category of symptom. However, the next psychiatrist found that this was a case of multiple personality and Milligan was hospitalized. To the ten personalities already enumerated, he now added ten others, including Adalana, an old lesbian, who had allegedly committed the rapes. Seeing this, the thousands of psychiatrists who drew up the DSM (thirty-eight thousand were involved in the preparation of DSM V) incorporated the new disorder into their classification of diseases.

A person, they said, may possess several quite distinct personalities, each with a name, a sex and a history that do not correspond to the sex, name and history of their host. These personalities appear suddenly in the course of daily life. They do so in the daytime and there is no need for the host-individual to be asleep. How do they show themselves? By a period of blankness, followed by amnesia. A blackout. A discreet trance, but a trance assuredly.

To identify the sixteen personalities inhabiting the patient Shirley/Sibyl, Dr Wilbur may have resorted to hypnosis and possibly to sodium pentothal. Transference was certainly involved.

It's the eternal scene all over again. In the role of the witches, Shirley and Billy. In the role of the exorcist, the therapists. In the role of the *parlements*, DSM III. And in the role of the Devil, a child abuser.

For in all the cases of multiple personality, the therapists discovered the cause—appalling abuse in childhood. How did they know this? In therapy, the memories came flooding back. And who were the abusers? The parents.

When subjected to attentive listening on the part of their therapists the multiple-personality patients began to describe real witches' sabbaths, orgies and child sacrifices. And just as a state machinery had gone into action to burn the sorcerer at Loudun, so an American-style legal machinery went into action to find the parents guilty of scandalous acts. The abused children (the vast majority were female) began legal actions against their parents.

And the parents were convicted. In 1992, coming together to defend and protect their children from this madness, a number of them created a False Memory Syndrome Foundation, to investigate memories induced by the therapists. One year later, three thousand families had joined the Foundation.

Following which, most logically, the allegedly abused children brought a complaint against their therapists for professional misconduct, accusing them of having manufactured false memories for them.

A whole string of witch trials.

It's not wrong to speak of witchcraft here, since American psychiatrists explicitly made the connection between multiple personalities and the incidence of demonic possession in past centuries. But instead of this affording them critical distance from the phenomenon, they drew the opposite conclusion and incorporated the long history of trance states in Europe into a future-oriented story, with demonic possession, hysteria and multiple personalities all confounded in the same long narrative, now assumed to be true.

In May 2010, the French subscription channel Canal Plus began broadcasting an American TV series called *The United States of Tara*, in which, after a firm decision to come out of medical treatment, the central character Tara Gregson (played by the astonishing Toni Collette) is possessed by five different personalities. Along with an alcoholic Vietnam veteran, an irritable adolescent boy and a five-year-old child, Tara's character is inhabited by a psychologist—better inside than out—and an uncontrollable animal personality. With her family around her, Tara gets by as best she can—an ordinary case of possession in ordinary times.

But the title is a stupefying one: *United States of Tara*. Tara, a sick woman, unites in her own person the multiple personalities of the USA.

A metaphor for an America prey to demons? At Salem Village, in 1692, twenty-five people were denounced by a group of girls who spoke unknown languages and 'slouched around' the streets. The individuals concerned were tried in the neighbouring town of Salem and sentenced to hanging for witchcraft. The accusations then grew so numerous that the region's economy slumped. The Boston clergy called for a halt to the procedures.

In 1953, the great writer Arthur Miller took up the story of the Salem witches once again, relating it to a witch-hunt then at its height: the Red Scare. On the say-so of Senator Joseph McCarthy, countless intellectuals and artists, including Charlie Chaplin, Marlene Dietrich and Bertolt Brecht were suspected of communism and blacklisted. The Red Scare came to an end when McCarthy rounded on the army and insulted a general. Censured by a vote in the senate, this latter-day Père Lactance died an alcoholic in 1957.

So, after Salem and McCarthy, witchcraft's third wave came in the form of the multiple-personality epidemic, a purely North American phenomenon (USA and Canada), rubber-stamped to a large extent by the third edition of the *Diagnostic and Statistical Manual of Mental Disorders*, its fifth edition as yet some way off.

There was nothing of the kind here in Europe. Despite the virulence of the debates between psychoanalysts and those among the neurologists who wanted to suppress the category, we've seen no epidemic of multiple personalities. Where are our trances, our rebellions? Have they completely disappeared? Do we still see any of these epidemics that affect only women and girls? Where does the trance lurk today?

CHAPTER 14

When the Body Goes into Eclipse
Instead of the Mind

After outlining the thinking of Freud, Babinski, Janet, Logre and Dumas, Dr Vinchon noted the fact that no attacks of hysteria were observed during the Great War. That nonsense had gone far enough.

In 1924, Vinchon drew the conclusion that hysteria was dying out.

In 1966, one world war later in a little room at the Sainte-Anne psychiatric hospital in Paris, I saw a girl assume the hysteric's 'crab position'. 'Her head was touching the ground and she was on the tips of her toes with her body thrown backwards in an arc', as the physicians treating the nuns of Loudun put it.

If I hadn't seen the incredible phenomenon with my own eyes, I wouldn't have sought high and low for the meaning and function of trance states. Had it not been for that disturbing sight, I wouldn't have written this book.

The therapist, André Green, a psychiatrist and psychoanalyst, waited impassively. The girl fell back inert on the ground. Then she got up and he showed her out. He didn't know much of the girl's personal history, since she'd fallen into this posture too soon for him to be able to explore it. But from what he did know, he proffered an explanation.

She'd got off the train at Montparnasse Station on her way to 'take up a position' as a maid in a middle-class household. She was from Brittany and had just arrived in Paris. As a country girl, she'd returned quite spontaneously to the old body postures—those from the repertoire of the demon-hunters and the nineteenth-century psychologists. It was an anachronistic symptom, a trace of the past.

That same year, at the Maison Blanche psychiatric hospital in Neuilly-sur-Marne, I found myself face to face with an old female patient labelled schizophrenic. She was walled up in herself, living—one arm raised—with what is known as 'waxy flexibility'. I could impress my thumb on her skin as though on a block of wax. The arm remained raised. Suddenly it relaxed and I received an impeccably delivered punch. For once in my life—I can't forget it—I was in the position of the exorcist, the psychiatrist, the demon-hunter, the tracker of memories. Has hysteria disappeared? Have trances disappeared?

Once I'd overcome my terror, I understood that the mind has total ascendancy over the body. It's capable of absolutely anything, except preventing it from dying. This is what the trance is for, because it cheats death.

When the trance is relegated to the realm of pathology, it finds pathways elsewhere, employing all possible means.

We have epidemics specific to girls today. Anorexia has taken the place of hysteria—ninety per cent of anorexics are girls.

They're obsessed with the idea of beauty and want a body without an ounce of fat. The means employed to lose weight are simple and violent: starving themselves, forcing themselves to vomit after eating, taking laxatives or enemas. In health terms, the results may be catastrophic: denutrition, decalcification, osteoporosis, the halting of the menstrual cycle, hair loss, reduced blood pressure, feelings of intense cold, dental disease, amnesia and, too often, suicide. A dangerous illness.

So are there no trances? Yes, there are. The violent coming and going of the alimentary bolus inside the body is a trance. Filling and emptying one's internal plumbing violently, making the abominable 'thing' enter and leave one's body is an imposed trance.

The facade is smooth, clean and neat, but the back-yard's dirty; it's where everything is flushed out, the site of glitches and stains. One side is a thing of the sublime, the other a thing of toilet bowls and flushing. What difference is there between Sister Stercophage and an anorexic? The one consumes excrement and spits out milk; the other consumes food and then spews it out, rejecting the excremental stage.

It's not surprising, then, that mental anorexia is extolled on the (now monitored) 'pro-ana' sites. Pro-ana is a title to be taken literally—long live anorexia! A pathology? No, a way of life, say those females who celebrate 'beauty' and 'perfection'. On a pro-ana site, you can find the tarantella of Apulia cited as a reference, with a photo of an arched body, a body twisted into a spider's shape. The heritage of the Apulian women and their spider bites isn't as dead as you might think.

Fasting is their way of life.

Who feels entitled to fast individually? A whole host of people. Female Christian saints in large numbers. Hindu ascetics, who are rumoured to be capable of extraordinary feats, such as the ascetic, cave-dwelling holy man of Madhya Pradesh who has eaten nothing for decades. And Jains who, when they come to the end of their life, begin a death fast. In the 1990s, you might have read in the press a first announcement that 'Mr X, a Jain, has begun his death fast today', and twelve days later, a second saying: 'Mr X parted from his body yesterday'.

The Greek gods also fast, if Jean-Pierre Vernant is to be believed: 'According to the Homeric formula, to enjoy imperishable life, to possess immortal blood (or not to have blood at all)' implies 'not to eat bread, not to drink wine'. And, where sacrifices prepared by human beings are concerned, 'this also means not to touch the flesh of the sacrificial victim, to keep for oneself only the aroma of the herbs burnt on the altar, the emanations of the charred bones that rise in smoke toward heaven.' And Vernant concludes that the Greek gods are always fasting ('*Les dieux grecs sont à jeun*').

This is the real desire—to live like the gods.

To be immortal. Is this possible? They want to achieve it. 'No way we're giving in,' you read on the websites, or 'pro-ana for a day, pro-ana forever'. Ginette Raimbault and Caroline Eliacheff have called them 'The Indomitables', in a book in which we find the same characters, the eternal fasters: the saints, the hysterics, a princess and an empress.

Elizabeth of Austria (Sissi), a rather chubby girl, showed her hysterical courage at the age of twenty-three by way of a presumed case of 'nervous consumption' with coughing and spitting of blood. These symptoms disappeared as soon as she was far away—on the island of Madeira—from the emperor, her husband. She had two daughters, one of whom died. A cruel mother-in-law and a deadly dull husband. The empress experienced a first eclipse. The anorexia nervosa began on her return, accompanied by daily athletic activity: endless barre exercises, walking and horse riding. The two forms of exercise and athleticism were the same: the aim was to tame the muscles, the bones, the digestion, the stomach—to tame things in general.

Taming the mind meant taming the emperor, that gentle donkey. Elizabeth wrote many poems on the subject, regarding them as so important that she bequeathed the royalties to the children of the political prisoners her husband the emperor had jailed.

And to tame the empire, she ran off, travelled, neglected her representative duties, boycotted the city of Vienna and lived not in Austria but elsewhere—on Corfu, in Normandy, in England, on ships or on her special train. If ever a sovereign knew how to eclipse herself politically, appearing and disappearing at Vienna and at Schönbrunn as the mood took her, she was that sovereign. The grandmother of contemporary anorexia nervosa, Sissi didn't waltz, didn't eat, had few loves in her life and didn't have sex. '*Toujours, toujours la chose génitale,*' said Charcot. A non-compliant body, stiffened in endless trance.

Dazzling, glorious, famed the world over, Sissi's figure remained the same to her dying day, as attested by the waist size of the bodice of black coarse-grained silk she was wearing on the day she was assassinated by an Italian anarchist at the age of sixty-one, as she ran to catch a steamer on Lake Geneva.

The empress didn't die of anorexia. Any more than Lady Di. Whereas the others die so much, princesses don't die of anorexia. Hence the slogan on a pro-ana site: 'We are all princesses.' And soon, goddesses.

It's no use women's magazines, which have now been alerted to the problem, choosing to celebrate chubby beauties with languorous thighs. The big couturiers press on with models known generically as 'girls'. Their masters aren't dressing women's bodies but the bodies of new-style human beings 'with tiny heads, long legs and arms that go on forever' (Karl Lagerfeld), bodies without hips or breasts. No smiles or any joy on their faces. That's how 'girls' are. Living dead with vampire faces.

In France, the turn of the twenty-first century saw another epidemic to terrify the mind—infanticidal women. In many cases it was a child born unexpectedly whose life was taken, since the woman was unaware that she was pregnant. Quiet women, good mothers and wives with no history of addiction, they're described as 'ordinary'. And there they are having killed their offspring.

This—mysterious—phenomenon demonstrates once again the power of the mind over the body. As an embryo is developing in her womb in an unusual vertical position, the woman beset by 'denial of pregnancy' puts on no weight, feels none of the foetus' movements and her figure doesn't change. And the fathers know nothing since there's nothing to see and nothing can be said.

Doctors attest how, immediately after the announcement of the pregnancy, the belly becomes rounded, sometimes between the examination couch and the doctor's desk. The child instantly acquires the place that was previously denied it. The pregnancy continues, the child is born and lives.

The term 'denial of pregnancy' is a distinctly recent one. In an age where contraception is easily available to women, the phenomenon seems disarmingly anachronistic. Can one really be pregnant without knowing it, ask worried girls? Pregnant and on the pill? Without feeling anything? This runs violently counter to the cult of 'His Majesty the Baby', the wanted child that all women desire.

Well, not all of them, clearly.

But strangling the child, suffocating it? Then putting it in the freezer and keeping it? In some cases, the courts didn't return a verdict of premeditation. So what view was actually taken? That you're not quite in your right mind when you've just given birth. A frantic rhythm, shaking, contractions, a bucking body, a massive force propelling the child outwards and lastly, a few spasms later, the expulsion of the afterbirth completes the bringing of the child into the world.

Afterbirth. This old word refers to the placenta which not so long ago was retained for cosmetic purposes; in other parts of the world, it was ritually buried beneath a tree dedicated to the child who'd just been born. In West Africa it's no joking matter, this afterbirth, this leftover portion which forms part of the child, since it is its double.

Freezing the dead child is perhaps of the same order. You're holding on to the soul.

But what have you done? Once the great convulsion is over, there's unimaginable disorder. Without any apparent pregnancy, what are these sticky remains issuing without warning from your womb? It's been born as if by magic. You're not quite in your right mind and your hands act on their own. You're possessed.

By what? 'I have trouble with the passing time,' says one of them.

In the time it took to make the nameless one disappear, she'd gone into eclipse.

CHAPTER 15

Gateways to the Body

Head

The eclipse strikes in the head, that's the privileged point of access. Migraines and vertigo mark the beginnings of a major disequilibrium. Or it may also be obsessive 'thinking', with the mind focussed on three drops of blood that abolish the world around them. Thinking cuts you off from the world and sends you at times into a trance.

In Benin and Togo, they make a little hole in the top of the skull to open a door to the vodun spirit. When the yogi in India sets about leaving his body, it's at the top of the skull, at the site of the fontanelle, that the ultimate ecstasy will occur that leads to the soul's escape. During cremation, after solemnly lighting the pyre, the son waits for the heat of the flames to make the skull explode. This is very clearly heard and those present shout, 'His soul is immortal!' because it has just departed his body.

Tongue

The tongue is often stuck out, broad and thick. This is the mark of the trance.

In the haka, the Maori warrior dance taken over by the All Blacks, New Zealand's rugby team, whose emblem is a silver fern leaf, two gestures indicate a combative trance: the quivering of the hands, a symbol of the scorching air that produces a shimmering effect, and the stuck-out tongue. For the enemy, this spells horror.

The stuck-out tongue signifies that the warrior opposite is in the grip of a force that sets him beside himself. He's in a trance, capable of anything.

The goddess Kali, who reigns over Bengal, sticks out a very long, very broad red tongue. With her necklace of decapitated heads, her skirt of severed arms and her tigress' fangs, she frightens the Whites but not the Bengalis who call her their Mother, adore her fierce appearance and the blood dripping from the limbs she turns into baubles.

Why do they love her so much?

Ramakrishna, who was recognized as a great mystic and a hero in Calcutta, where he has been worshipped since the nineteenth century, so loved Kali that he wanted at all costs to achieve ecstasy with his beloved Mother. But to no avail. He found the practice of yoga difficult, had unsuccessfully attempted the rite of tantric union with a yogi woman and, turning from Kali, had even attached a monkey's tail to his bottom to change his human body into that of Hanuman, the divine monkey . . .

Until the day when, maddened with despair and furious at his failures, Ramakrishna pulled out a sword in the temple and threatened to kill himself in front of the statue of Kali. At that moment he received illumination, was enfolded in infinite waves of emotion and found himself dissolved into his beloved. By this suddenness we recognize the trance state, different from the ecstasy he had been unable to attain by classical means.

Born into a family of very poor Brahmans, the boy who was to become Ramakrishna had experienced his very first eclipse in a field at the age of five: in a sky black with heavy monsoon clouds, he had seen a flight of cranes whose whiteness stood out brilliantly against the stormy background. He fell down thunderstruck. Then he took off in pursuit of marvels and wonders.

From the moment he raised his sword against his adored mother, the crazed lover of Kali had visions. He provided the formula for these: 'Meow, meow.' These are his own words. He went into prolonged periods of ecstasy, some lasting for six months. These can be seen in a photograph that shows him standing, eyes half-closed, arm upraised, with enormous lips drawn out in the fearsome smile of Kali. Such love!

Admittedly, the monsteress was created by gods who had come together to free the earth from threatening demons—like the *bonae dominae*, Kali is redemptive. But she isn't content with just her bloody costume; from time to time she even beheads herself and her severed head's mouth avidly drinks the blood spurting from her own neck . . . And in this guise she tramples on a love-making couple.

Ordinarily, when she isn't drinking, Kali is still trampling a man's body, a white body.

She tramples, she stamps. With her long black hair standing up on the top of her head, she dances. Kali is a goddess in a warlike trance, akin in this to the Maori warriors in their ritual combat. Her dance is so wild that this was how she inadvertently trampled the body of one of her begetters, the god Shiva, beneath her fearsome feet. A Yogi scholar told me with a smile that the goddess Kali felt such shame when she realized her mistake that she stuck out her tongue—oops—and stopped.

The orthodox version of this stuck-out tongue is much more technical. Each morning yogis slowly cut away at the string (the *fraenum*) which attaches the tongue to the back of the palate with the edge of a cutting grass. Each day the tongue lengthens. One day, it is free. It can touch the end of the nose or the chin. There's a purpose to this exercise—to achieve a major convulsion, the yogi can then turn his tongue around in the back of his throat and die of suffocation.

Kali's stuck-out tongue is the tongue of a yogini, a yogi woman who has passed this point and cut away the *fraenum*. She doesn't give a damn, she's dancing, she's in a trance.

The Convulsionary version: women demand to have their tongues pierced, split crosswise, pounded.

The exorcists' version: a woman possessed can be recognized by her tongue being stuck out, thick and black. She's a provincial Kali.

The pornographic version: from the fifteenth to the eighteenth centuries, witches stick their tongues out obscenely, like actresses in X-rated movies. Like the restless forked tongue of a snake.

Nostrils

The nose is used for breathing. In yoga, you never breathe by raising the rib cage but always abdominally. This is the first thing the learner acquires. To empty his mind completely of thoughts—the primary aim of yoga—the yogi suspends his breathing by stopping up first one nostril, then the other in a calculated rhythm. This is the best path for achieving a positive ecstasy. The ideal is to stop breathing.

But the nose has many other functions. It attests to the presence of perfumes or, alternatively, of stinking odours. And since it has the eminent role of smell detector, the nose also serves a great deal for sneezing. When satisfied, the wandering womb makes women sneeze. In trances, or when cocaine is sniffed, you sneeze. The trance of a Siberian shaman ends with a sneeze—the supernatural spirit has departed.

Elsewhere, the sneeze opens up a little door for it. While she was preparing to enter the dance, the trance-mistress of the Dakar region gave out a powder to her aides that was to be stuffed into the nostrils to facilitate the arrival of the spirits. I tried this.

It was a little bit like snuff—just a little peppery, bitter, pleasant. And nothing happened. The trance-mistress waited. After a few minutes I succumbed to a violent fit of sneezing. 'That's to purify you,' she said with much laughter, since I couldn't provide a home for a spirit from the ocean depths.

Mouth

The mouth is used for vomiting substances and words. Blackish substances, rotting cadaverous matter, obscenities, imaginary languages or languages that have not been learnt, like the Tupinamba spoken by a Loudun nun or the baby talk of the Convulsionary sisters. The anorexic mouth opens to regurgitate the substances ingested under the pressure of hunger. Then, closed, cleaned, its paint refreshed, it makes some beautiful smiles.

In trances, the mouth has no one it might address in the language being spoken all around it. The mouth speaks to its gods, its spirits, its devils and its animals.

To eclipse yourself in a trance you have to know how to vomit. To wait for a child to arrive too. There's no vomiting in the denial of pregnancy but there certainly is in phantom pregnancies.

Viscera

The belly is a vulnerable place. That's where the rotting of the body begins after death. This great site for blowflies, scavenger beetles, nematodes, oribatid mites, myriapods, collembola—these 'obscure death workers' labouring upon the body—is so feared by human beings that they go to enormous lengths to avoid seeing it.

Putting yourself in a state of apparent death by means of a lethargic sleep or the demented inertia that follows convulsions is a good idea; the idea of playing dead. The way animals do when attacked by their predators.

Though the abdominal muscles can be transformed into armour-plating, though peristaltic movements can be regulated by breathing, and though good excretion can be ensured and you can see to the proper functioning of the internal organs, no exercise can slow the stomach's decomposition.

The witchcraft attacks of African 'cannibals' are often directed against the belly, but trances will not come through it. This is why the ritual collection of excrement has such importance—it is evacuated life.

Foot and Leg

The feet are subject to inflexible constraints. Since, to avoid pollution from pigs, not the slightest suspicion of leather is allowed, nor plastic, because you never know if cows were involved, when you enter a mosque or a

Hindu, Jain or Sikh temple—and, by an effect of conta-
gion, a Christian church in India—you do so with bare
feet. And the feet are bare when you dance on the sand.
The point is to make contact with the ground through
the conductive sole of the foot.

By contrast, a shaman must be shod in shoes from the
pelt of his deer, with stag's legs. No shaman without shoes.

Constructing his winding path through the
shamanic regions from Ireland to Siberia, Ginzburg
reminds us that the Greek heroes often had need of sandals to face up to monsters. He writes of the two gilded
sandals like his father's that Theseus finds under a rock;
Perseus' single sandal given by the god Hermes for fighting the Gorgon; and that other one for Jason before the
meeting with his wicked uncle. Before committing suicide, Dido, Queen of Carthage, removes one of her sandals; Medea does the same to invoke Hecate, the funereal
goddess. And the swollen feet from which Oedipus gets
his name may perhaps recall an initiation whose ritual
has been forgotten.

One single bare foot is something that brings us
closer to death. For example, allowing one's leg to be
bared on one side is a simulation of the passage through
death. We find it in the Masonic rite when the initiate
has to show his courage and be prepared for the worst.

When it comes to passing over to the other side of
life, asymmetry is to be preferred. With one foot shod
and the other bare, you limp but you are strong. For
example, as a result of having wrestled all night with the
angel, Jacob had a hip put out of joint and received the
name of 'Israel', the one who fights with God.

This altercation with God inspired Paul Claudel's *Le
Soulier de satin* (1929; *The Satin Slipper*, 1931), a drama
divided into four separate days and set in the Age of

Discovery, at a time when the conquistadors are showing their first signs of remorse. In it, the author sends his mystical heroine off into the forbidden lands of adulterous love but, before she yields, she doffs a slipper which she offers up to the Virgin Mary: '. . . when I venture to make a leap into evil, let me do so with a limp!'

The murderous rite of the stumbling Bacchantes on the island opposite Nantes was carried out in Greece in a more peaceable form as the 'dance of the crane', with one foot gracefully raised and held before being set down again.

In present-day Greece, not far from Salonika, the Anastenaria ritual is performed, with both sexes involved. Feet dance on the embers, marking out a cross in them. Once the fire is out and the rite over, the devil has been vanquished and the sick, blind, deaf and nervously ill have been cured. Rain can even be summoned. And the refrain is always one of rest and well-being: 'No woman was ever as sweet as the fire this evening,' an Anastenaride tells an ethnologist.

Who are the Anastenarides? They are Greek emigrants, orthodox Christians who came from Bulgaria in 1912, bringing with them their icon of Saint Constantine and Saint Helena combined on the same wooden panel. France Schott-Billmann rightly explains how the Emperor Constantine, who remained a sun-worshipper, retains features of Alexander the Great, if not indeed of Herakles, who was half-man, half-god. As for Helena his mother, she found the 'true' cross of Christ and those of the two robbers. Venerated now as a queen and a mother, Saint Helena was a servant-concubine when a general impregnated her with the future emperor.

It is she the Anastenarides hail before crying 'Long live Greece!' as they rush forward, red kerchiefs in hand, to walk on the fire.

Before going off to trace out a cross on the flaming embers, there is frantic dancing in front of the icon. People carry it in their arms and a butcher is called upon to slit the throat of a bull, whose blood spills onto the earth. The consecrated animal is then skinned and its meat cut into pieces to be eaten. The fire is lit and the company waits for night to fall. Then, when the fire subsides and the embers are glowing, they set off in procession with the musicians, and the *archianastenaris*, the master of the rite, hails Greece, brandishes the icon and leaps onto the fire, marking out the first cross. This takes place today—and in the European Union.

But let's move outside the magical geography traced out by Ginzburg and take a look at the best known of empire-founding African heroes. Sundiata Keita, born in 1190 in present-day Guinea, was paralysed in both legs until the age of seven and lived with his mother in poverty and contempt. All of a sudden, he acquired the ability to walk and, showing fearsome strength, rid himself of his enemies and founded the Empire of Mali.

To Sundiata's recovery, to the strength of the hero when he is born a cripple, we may properly add the animals resuscitated by Madonna Oriente, who struck the bag of skin containing the bones of the oxen that had just been eaten and revived them at a stroke.

All the bones. And Fairest One is careful when gathering up the bones of her brother Clever, killed by an old witch. All of them have to be there for the resurrection. If one is missing . . .

The bones of the paschal lamb aren't broken, nor are the legs of the crucified Christ; the son of God must remain intact. In an operation of shamanic magic, if a bone happens to be missing for a man's resurrection, it is replaced by a branch or twig or even by the bone of the dog that ate the man's bone. And if a sandal is missing, then Cinderella will be off balance as she comes down the palace staircase.

Ginzburg suggests correlations between the single sandal, the twisted or naked leg, the animals whose bones are gathered together and the bag of skin they're wrapped up in. 'Metamorphoses, cavalcades, ecstasies, followed by the egress of the soul in the shape of an animal—these are different paths to a single goal. Between animals and souls, animals and the dead, animals and the beyond, there exists a profound connection.' So, we are going to see death—this is what trances do. See it to avoid it, deceive it, charm it. In this gigantic geography which Ginzburg sees extending as far as Siberia, animals—the familiars of spirits—are the vectors of the journey into the beyond.

The bare, raised foot is the one you make ready to leave with, like poor Dido in the moment of her suicide. But the bag of skin?

In shaman country, to be born with a caul affords you second sight. You're born 'with a caul' when the bag of waters doesn't break and the child presents itself in protected form, surrounded by its amniotic sac. It's a sign of luck. Even into our own day, the amniotic 'caul' will be preserved, dried out and clung to, as a lucky charm. Like the placenta, which has served to nourish the child, the amniotic sac that has protected the foetus isn't a waste product to be thrown in the bin but a bag of skin that brings blessings, a protective material.

Unsurprisingly, a large number of funeral ceremonies prescribe that the dead person should be sewn into a skin, the equivalent of our first membrane and a good insurance for resurrection. Veiling the deceased or wrapping them in a winding-sheet is scarcely any different. Why do we wrap them up? Clearly to protect them from the dark, subterranean banquet.

Horns

They will tell you in West Africa—in southern Senegal to be precise—that, 'We haven't practised human sacrifice for a long time. We've replaced human beings with hornless black bull-calves.' But that, say others, is what they used to call the human victims.

Young animals whose horns haven't grown yet, with bulging brows covered in ringlets.

The Buryat Exirit-Bulagat tribe venerate a horned founder, His Lordship the Bull. He's the son of the heavens who fell to earth in the shape of a blue bull, to meet the challenge of a speckled one belonging to a human being.

The animals fight, gore each other and the blue bull is about to win out when the daughter of the speckled bull's owner weakens the blue one with her menstrual blood. Furious, the bull impregnates her. At the birth, he places the newborn between his horns, tosses it with a shake of his head and brings it up in the place where it falls.

This is how the epic of the Exirit-Bulagat begins. In conclusion, the blue bull, father of a heavenly child, but defeated by defilement from a woman, is turned to stone on a mountain peak where he remains to this day.

The reindeer breeders have a consecrated reindeer, the cattle breeders a consecrated bull. Alongside the sessions involving trances, the shamans engage in 'goring games' for ritual festivals, weddings or to relax the audience after a rather rough session. Wearing their horned head-dresses with reindeer antlers, they 'shamanize', calling up the spirits and, in the case of His Lordship the Bull—even though they aren't wearing its horns but those of the reindeer—they get down on all fours, bellow, scratch at the ground with one hand and, in the end, gore each of the participants in the assembly in turn, striking them in the belly to bring them fertility. The young boys wrestle head to head and, before fighting, the adult wrestlers throw a handful of sand and scratch at the ground like bulls.

Let's now cross the Bering Strait and move to North America. In 1876, a famous Hunkpapa shaman, at the head of a coalition of the Sioux peoples, had a vision: white soldiers were falling in great numbers, like raindrops, from the sky. Sitting Bull's vision occurred on 25 June, the day the leader of the Seventh Cavalry, Colonel Custer—a veteran campaigner of the 'Indian Wars', known familiarly as 'Hard Ass'—was killed at the Battle of Little Big Horn, the only Native American victory over white American troops who lost two hundred fifty officers and men. And the white soldiers fell like raindrops.

But Sitting Bull's vision hadn't come spontaneously. When the 'Father of All', Ulysses Simpson Grant, the great white president of Washington, had issued an ultimatum to all the Sioux peoples to quit the land of the Black Hills on 31 January 1876, their shaman began the Sun Dance.

Pins were driven into his back muscles with leather straps attached and a heavy bison skull was tied to them. The shaman began to dance, dragging behind him the skull, its horns ploughing up the earth. Sitting Bull danced for three days and nights. He stared straight into the sun until he was dazzled by it and his vision came to him.

After his victory, Sitting Bull took off to Canada and eventually surrendered. On his liberation, he became one of the stars of Buffalo Bill's 'Wild West Show'. The banned Sun Dance reappeared under the name Ghost Dance and in 1890 Sitting Bull was shot down for supporting it.

Bodily ordeals exert a drug-like attraction. In *Résistance à l'effacement* the ethnologist Ralf Marsault photographed Berlin's punks in the 1990s and reported the experiences of his friend Soubi who went off to South Africa to take part in a body-art performance.

Soubi had his skin pierced with hooks spread out over the surface of his body. These were then raised with pulleys.

Soubi felt no pain. He felt well and warm and could no longer feel his body. His vision came to him: the hooks had become stars in the sky and he had flown off like an arrow . . . 'as in the early morning in the swamplands it was warm, there was water and everything was fine'.

Margaret Murray, who was born in Calcutta in 1863 and lived to be a hundred, was working as an Egyptologist when she believed she'd discovered the existence of a pre-Christian fertility cult in Europe which venerated the 'Horned God'. One of her starting points was the famous prehistoric image drawn on the walls of the Three Brothers Cave in Ariège.

This is called 'the Sorcerer' and depicts a figure half-stag half-man. It has enormous testicles, sports two antlers and is pictured face-on to the viewer. It is the ritually sacrificed Horned God, a god that was worshipped, according to Murray, right up to the fifteenth century.

No one in the academic community now lends credence to Murray's arguments. She deduced her description of the cult of the Horned God from confessions made by women the Inquisition assumed to be witches, transforming those confessions into unequivocal facts. This is the criticism Ginzburg levels against her, though he does admit she had discovered 'a kernel of truth', which he refers to as shamanism 'from Ireland to Asia'.

As one of the manifestations of the Horned God—a sacrificial victim offering itself to human beings—Murray identified Joan of Arc who was born in Lorraine, a region where women were followers of the witch cult of Diana or Herodias, a place of trees and fairies. These fairies spoke to her and Joan followed their 'voices' until, as a good pagan, she was ritually sacrificed.

In accordance with this logic, Gilles de Rais, fellow warrior of the Maid of Orleans, did nothing to save her, knowing she was giving herself as a sacrifice as the 'old religion' demanded. He later followed suit, allowing himself to be accused of the most heinous crimes. Joan and Gilles de Rais were burnt as sorcerers.

As a result, the Catholic Church might be thought, in 1920, to have canonized a pagan woman, long after it excommunicated her pagan companion.

This kindly rehabilitation of the Devil enjoyed great success. I cannot help but think that Murray, having spent her childhood in Calcutta, a city where young she-goats are guillotined daily in Kali's honour, had become accustomed to young goats and bloody sacrifices.

As painted by Goya in the moonlight, El gran cabrón (The Great He-Goat) sits up on his haunches and has pride of place in a circle of women of all ages, one of whom is holding a child. His lyre-shaped horns have a sprinkling of foliage on them, and he is keenly eyeing the shoulders of one of the women in the ring. He is thinking of Rosemary who will bear his son in *Rosemary's Baby* (1968), the film by Roman Polanski, a survivor of the Cracow ghetto and a man familiar with witch-hunts.

CHAPTER 16

The Disciplines of Fear

Overseen within rigorous rules, an eclipse achieved through a trance unfolds and ends without any great drama; the assistants see to this.

When no rules are set for it, a trance rages wildly, running to extremes after the fashion of the Convulsionaries. To go and take a close look at death requires your being able to return from it in a disciplined way.

At Dakar, during the 'dance' hours, a dozen or so girls went into spontaneous trances: screams, howls, arched bodies, chaotic gestures. A minute later, they were passed from one set of arms to another, then taken out to the treatment station. At the next ceremony, their initiation would be undertaken. This unscripted trance announced their entry into the world of spirits. It would be unthinkable not to monitor a girl experiencing some kind of attack during the dance. And this is as true for the Lébou of the Dakar region as for the *tarantati* of Apulia in their day.

To initiate is to treat the dangerous moments of life's transitions with strict rules.

Being born from the womb is the first transition; but the unfinished child has to be completed, transformed into a person and integrated into her people, group and country. This is what Christian baptism does, removing the child from Limbo and non-existence.

Dying is the last transition and, just as the unfinished child has to be completed, so the dead person must be completed, transformed into an ancestor, incorporated into the hosts of the dead, guided towards his new country.

Whereas in Africa this passage into death may take several years, with us it has shrunk to almost nothing. We flush away the dead person. A trapdoor opens, the coffin disappears, we wait and wait without even a hint of ceremony and an urn comes back to us in its stead. The same word—incineration—is used to describe the process for disposing of domestic waste and the process for disposing of a body that was alive. And what becomes of the dead man? Dust was his name.

Of the two, the most dangerous transition is the one that transforms children's bodies into adult ones, a prodigious mutation that causes hair to grow, sperm to spurt and blood to flow; that gives girls breasts and boys a different voice. It's difficult to leave these young people to their own devices at such a disconcerting time. But what will we do if we have no initiation?

All initiations of the young—girls or boys—involve a carefully supervised violence. The metaphorical demand in initiation is for the adolescent to pass through death and be subsequently re-born, but this is a mere trifle by comparison with the rigours imposed in the countries of the Gulf of Guinea, Brazil or the Caribbean, where the rite of passage is well established. There we find confinement, darkness, drugs, scarification, markings of the body, the learning of languages and songs.

Hazing—uncontrolled and dangerous—is outlawed now in France. The ordeal of the baccalaureate remains, that last tiny rite which the media try manfully each year to transfigure into extreme emotion when the results come out.

Observing a major epidemic of drugs, petty criminality and, in particular, defenestration among many boys and girls of African background living among us, the ethnopsychologist Tobie Nathan has come to the conclusion that, in drugging themselves or throwing themselves out of windows for no apparent reason, these young people aren't trying to commit suicide but are suffering from a lack of fear.

Zahra, a twenty-nine-year-old Kabyle woman, is on heroin—one fix a day. Her very worried mother takes her to the Devereux Centre, which treats migrants with major problems, often at the bidding of a judge. Zahra's mother speaks very good French; she's integrated and has transformed herself perfectly. Eighteen years into that transformation she felt homesick. She wanted to see her mother again—and the sun and Kabylia . . . Her family went there on holiday. And it was from that time on that her daughter Zahra began to change.

At birth Zahra was given the name of her sister, a first child who had died of 'green diarrhoea'. However integrated she might be into her Parisian life, her mother was convinced that the first Zahra died as a result of the 'evil eye' of a woman who had stared too long at the child.

The second Zahra, the drug-taker, wears an eye-shaped pendant round her neck, which people all round the Mediterranean rim regard as good protection.

Why does Zahra take drugs? 'To manufacture herself,' says Nathan. Because she had a twofold metamorphosis to perform—because she had to be both herself and her dead sister and remain a Kabyle while living in Paris—the girl Zahra sought out an agent capable of helping her to transform herself. 'The drug had acted like an emigration, enabling her to experience both its sense of strangeness and contradictory feelings,' writes Nathan, the founder of the Devereux Centre.

In unwittingly repeating her mother's history, as Nathan sees it, Zahra evokes the god Dionysus. Before being the god of trances and wine, the child Dionysus lived under threat. Despite the protection of the Corybantes, he was captured. On the orders of the jealous Hera, the Titans tore him limb from limb and boiled up the pieces. Rhea, the earth goddess, put him back together again.

Dismembering and reassembling is one of the operations involved in initiation. Initiation requires—purposely frightening—traumatic techniques, using strong emotions as a lever. It makes marks on the body in some of those parts that are entranceways for the trance. Lastly, it isn't immediately understandable and provides no explanation.

Fright, markings and enigmatic ordeals are all involved.

Since she's a hybrid being, torn between the Kabyle village community and the French education system, drugs didn't supply Zahra with the transformative agent she was looking for, for want of a support system and 'constructed' fright. 'So there she is, caught in the toils of the drug, since a toxin without a new world to invade forms a world of its own,' concludes Nathan, before going on to relate other tragic stories.

Blanche, whose parents are from Martinique, believes herself to be bewitched. She jumps from the seventeenth storey and—merely—breaks both her legs. At the age of twelve, Fatiha, a well-integrated Kabyle girl, sees a woman in traditional costume who tells her in the Kabyle language that her parents are waiting for her downstairs. She jumps from the third floor, breaking her arms and legs.

These are all logics of second births that will have to be re-begun alone, in individual questings after fear, without assistants to ease the passage to adulthood. And this is still going on. In the night of 22 to 23 October 2010, twelve people, including seven children, threw themselves out of the second-floor window of a council block in the Yvelines. A baby died as a result. Though confused, the witnesses' various versions indicated that two of the women had joined an evangelical church fanatically committed to purification. Their parents were born in Central Africa.

Supervised fear builds and structures resilient human beings. Lacking the rites of their countries of origin, these adolescents are trying desperately to reconstruct them in wildcat form: so as to experience fear, they jump.

Is this the imposed fear of a simulated death? No, it's something else. Admittedly, the initiate is sometimes forced into a dark place—into a tunnel dug in the earth, for example. Or he's locked in a darkened room so that he cannot see. These things are frightening.

But often the aim is to achieve a thorough regression to the animal state: in Benin's vodun, in Haiti's voodoo or in Bahia's candomblé, the initiates—drugged boys and girls—eat like animals and drink from dog bowls.

We're back with animals again at the decisive moment, when the initiates, male and female, drink the warm liquid that pours from the severed neck of the bird above their heads. You've played at being an animal, now you're drinking the animal.

You've passed through fear.

To cleave the spirit to the body of the initiate, the trance-mistress I saw at Dakar carefully applied the blood of the sacrificed animals to the tiniest patch of bare skin, working from top to bottom. She then wiped it away with a live cockerel, using its feathers as a sponge.

Her movements were gentle and the initiates remained calm. The animals' blood served as an emergency skin and only the officiant drank it warm from the bull's throat during the sacrifice. She took the fear upon herself.

Once the fright is past, the initiates begin work. They are taught new and secret languages or ways of singing in high voices, like the little girls from an initiation 'convent' in Benin whose singing so charmed Gilbert Rouget near Porto-Novo in 1969.

There were some sixty girls in the group, aged between two and fourteen, who were engaged in a solemn 'coming-out' at the end of their initiation. These 'new ones' had to form a procession to go and hail the king. Their shaven heads covered with pearls, their shoulders freshly scarified and oiled, their torsos crossed by two great belts of cowrie shells and rings about their ankles, they walked quickly, looking at no one, occasionally striking up a marching song that was brisk but, says the ethnologist, 'tinged with a certain sadness'.

When they had reached the palace and been admitted to the king's presence, they bowed down before him and sang for twenty minutes. The king greeted them, their instructor translated his words into the secret language and they responded with a thanksgiving. The remarkable beauty of these songs, which we know from the recordings made by Rouget, gives full meaning to the notion of a silvery voice, lying as it does between the tinkling of crystal glasses, the glockenspiel and the exercises of a coloratura soprano singing softly to herself. These initiates sang with 'supernatural' voices.

They weren't in their normal state, says Rouget. Behaving like automata, with lifeless eyes, and not understanding everyday language—the king's words had to be translated for them—they were in the kind of stupor known in Africa as *omotum* and in Brazil as *ere*. They weren't people possessed either, for there was no jerking about, no spasms, no hint of a convulsion or cry. They were in a state of 'dispossession'.

Rouget gives this description. 'Anyone who has seen "fetishists" in Dahomey cannot have failed to notice a particular kind of reserve, of dignity that radiates from them, an inner bearing, as it were, that is different from that of ordinary people, a quiet energy that emanates from them and distinguishes them from everyone else. The long initiation they had to undergo must certainly have produced a very special ripening of their personality ... [T]here is every reason to suppose the novices emerge from this ordeal at least partly transformed.'

While undergoing this transformation, the girls were in a trance, in one of those discreet, barely perceptible trances, eclipses that run smoothly and involve no shouting but nonetheless entail leaving the body in the best and safest way.

Such are the trances of the believers who come to hear the qawwali singers in the Sufi sanctuaries of India: they remain seated, the upper half of their bodies gently swaying, though, seen from close to, their eyes are rolled upwards. They return, rosy-cheeked, to their senses, before rising to shower bank notes down on the heads of the singers, scattering the money—that absolute Nothing—with a broad gesture.

In an initiation, work is done on the skin. It is pierced and coloured, cut and incised. Bits of flesh are cut off. A tiny hole is made in the skin at the top of the skull and objects are inserted into the cartilage of the nose or the ears. When the work is over, the initiates wear their finished, scarred, ineradicable marks of belonging on their skin.

In our world this spells danger. We know how the Nazis lowered the trousers of Jewish men and boys to find their circumcised victims. We know how, subsequently, they tattooed strings of figures on the arms of the women and men doomed to extermination, conferring a new identity in the accountancy of death. Do those adolescents of today know this, who work on their skin, having it tattooed, scarified and pierced to insert metallic objects into places both sensitive and insensitive?

With us, work done on the skin is subject to controls. Tattooing and piercing is performed by professionals and there are rules for these things, relating strictly to the health aspect. But the symbolic rules aren't fixed at all. They're fluid and hazy.

The bodily manufacture of belonging, without initiation, reconnects with some old models. This is the case in prisons, where 'families' are created, or with Stephenie Meyer's new vampires. You change species, you're another type of human. You alone create yourself as member of a group. This was the—very free—desire of the punks whose doings were recorded by Ralf Marsault. Scarified, tattooed, sporting highly decorated costumes that were improvised each day, and using animal skulls or gas masks as ornaments, they seem to have passed through a period of wildcat initiation, inventing a set of rules for themselves.

Admittedly, they didn't eat much and they drank a lot. Nor was their hygiene beyond reproach. But these nomadic, welcoming communities, in which young drifters from all over Europe settled for a few years, had an ideal—the family and family therapy. They formed a family and that was the main thing. They invented their own rite—a drunken dance in which one of them, throwing him- or herself from a stage, surfed from arm to arm above an ocean of heads, incurring no bodily harm. They assisted one another as a group and help was available.

Berlin has been renovated from top to bottom and the punks eradicated. Only their memory remains, as is indicated by the title of the book *Résistance à l'effacement* (Resistance to Obliteration, 2010).

When things are eradicated, madness often rules in their stead. When, on Louis XIV's orders, the abbey of Port-Royal-des-Champs had been razed to the ground, the frenzy of the Convulsionaries began. Once health and safety rules outlawing all danger have been enacted, the invention of new rites begins in disorderly fashion.

We've seen this burning desire for initiation everywhere. Among the nuns who marked themselves with red-hot irons; in the animal postures of the possessed; in the budding shamans' flights into the forest; in the contemplation of the three droplets of blood of a wild goose on the white of the snow; in changes of voice, gender and species. In Tristan and Iseult's goblet of wine—'herbed', drugged wine.

To desire these eclipses is *just* to change life.

But 'just' implies something terrifying—with ironclad rules to overcome fear. Uncontrolled, this desire for eclipse becomes excessive and destructive. Our world is haunted. To mutilate yourself by cutting strips of flesh from your skin; to knock yourself out massively and hurriedly with alcohol so that you fall straight into the state so well described as 'dead drunk'; to gather together, with music and drugs, so as to form one single body with a host of other people—these are wildcat initiations, manufacturings of fears bereft of the attendant knowledge. This isn't 'just'.

Binge drinking—getting hugely, instantaneously drunk—is a dangerous eclipsing of life. Otherwise, it's not done right and it's not an eclipse. The subject has to disappear and the trance state must prevail. But there's no safety-net to this dangerous activity.

The eclipse may suddenly occur as *raptus*, when consciousness is abruptly snatched away. It happens, indeed, that people kill themselves by eclipsing themselves from life. It's even crossed my mind at times that the harrowing mass phenomenon of suicides in the workplace, caused by excess of authority and the hounding of employees—particularly at the Renault factories—has to do with these eclipses from life. Admittedly, the motive is to be sought in an inhuman demand for profitability and these sudden eclipses are the product of long rumination, but at the last moment, in the workplace, they become absolutely compelling as if in a dream or, rather, a trance. A compulsion to throw oneself over a guard rail, to hurl oneself from a great height, to fall out of life.

Now, if it isn't to be dangerous, the trance has need of an attentive, benevolent circle of people around it. It's a learning process with teachers. This is why, down Dakar way, there will always be possessed women refusing the spirits access to their bodies so that they can take care of the others.

Without the disciplining of fright, the trance doesn't lead on to a metamorphosis. When disciplined, it enables you to change species or gender.

But why animals? Why do all trances have a moment of barking, lowing or yelping—including those gatherings driven to wild frenzy by the voice of Hitler?

In small hunter-gatherer societies or in regions where cattle or deer are bred, animals are neighbours to human beings and it's understandable they should be vehicles for the trance. In the rural France where the Loudun possessions took place, animals were still kept in locations very close to the town. In Paris at the Saint-Médard convent, it was the charnel-house that was most significant—the trance convulsions were seen in the heart of the graveyard, and yet animals still appeared either in the cries uttered or in the form of people going about on all fours.

Animals were there all the time.

At the end of the nineteenth century, Ramakrishna mews for his goddess in the capital of the Indian Empire, Calcutta, a major city. At the beginning of the twenty-first century, women in Africa become chameleons and snakes in a capital city with a million inhabitants. And in Northern France, a woman who is accusing a priest of paedophilia rushes on all fours behind the chair of the examining magistrate. The trance animal hasn't disappeared.

When it comes to thinking through the question of the inner animal, Freud doesn't hold back. *Civilization and Its Discontents* (1930), based entirely on an evolutionist argument that past ages return as a prehistoric 'repressed', is a thorny text. Considering the question of the vividness of smells, which were so powerful among his dear hysterics, Freud comes out squarely, in one of his footnotes, with a conclusion.

At a certain point, he tells us, human beings stopped going on all fours and walked upright, moving away from the ground. From this vertical posture two consequences ensue.

First, when standing, men and women uncover their genital organs, which were previously hidden, and the genesis of the sense of shame ensues. Here you might think you were reading the Bible.

Second, olfactory stimuli are 'devalued', conceding precedence to visual ones. The organs of smell are now further away from the genitals.

Then, after a long passage on excrement, which isn't found disgusting by the child but is distasteful to the adult who has been taught cleanliness, Freud suddenly fires off on the subject of dogs.

> A person who is not clean—who does not hide his excreta—is offending other people; he is showing no consideration for them. And this is confirmed by our strongest and commonest terms of abuse. It would be incomprehensible too that man should use the name of his most faithful friend in the animal world—the dog— as a term of abuse if that creature had not incurred his contempt through two characteristics: that it is an animal whose dominant sense is that of smell and one which has no horror of excrement, and that it is not ashamed of its sexual functions.

To translate into everyday language, dogs smell the anuses of their fellows, sniff their turds and mount other dogs, male or female, at every opportunity.

In Christian lands haunted by the question of witches, the odours of sanctity or of musk roses might be said then, quite simply, to be the reverse of anal smells. With a simple, 'animal' logic.

Elsewhere, however, animals have a different status. In shamanic lands, whether in Siberia or among the Amerindians in America, or in all those regions that think in animistic terms, the animal is a relative of human beings.

It is treated as such. When, after asking its permission, an animal is killed in a hunt, the young of that animal are gathered up afterwards and raised with the children; they are fed like babies and treated when they are ill. And when they die, their funeral is celebrated as a human being's would be. Do animists really 'think' like this? That isn't the point. Like the question of simulation in trances, this question 'drops out'.

Animistic thinking doesn't separate animals from human beings as we do. In trances, the animists aren't changing worlds but simply their outer garments; and the beyond is inside them whereas it is not inside us.

After living among the Achuar Indians of the Jivaroan group, the ethnologist Philippe Descola calls the animals and plants that share the world with humans 'non-humans'. In the shaman's trance, they're not external, alien beings but alter egos that are 'invited to lend their aid', as can be seen from the scene of the 'rutting-reindeer' shaman.

Makanch was one of a pack of dogs of a woman whose job was to prepare the dogs for the men's hunt and Anne-Christine Taylor, the wife of Descola, was helping her with that task.

Makanch was a laggard, inclined to be lazy. She was a reluctant hunter. To remedy this, her mistress administered a large dose of Jimson weed (*datura stramonium*) which is used by the Achuar to make contact with their spirits.

Invariably it is because he has killed an enemy that an Achuar has to go off to meet his 'vision', to renew his vital force which is weakened by the act of taking a human life. This vision—*arutam*—is obtained by swallowing tobacco juice and *datura stramonium*, a plant containing high levels of scopolamine. Then, in the solitude of the forest, the vision is heralded by a great wind that brings out the monstrous animal—giant jaguar, entwined anacondas, dismembered bodies. The man must hold out his hand and touch this thing. Then the apparition disperses and, when calm is restored, the *arutam*, the Ancient one, arises and delivers a soothing message.

Under the influence of the *datura*, the dog began to spin round, to stagger about terror-stricken, unsteady on its feet. It was in a trance, writes Descola. Like a human.

When one day I asked Anne-Christine what the dog Makanch had been changed into in the trance, her answer came quick as a flash. Into a jaguar. The dog too could go into a trance and shift from one life to another. Makanch too had found *arutam*.

The myths Lévi-Strauss brings together in *Mythologics* (1964–76) all speak of a time of origins as a world without differentiation between animals and human beings, a world in which the 'non-humans' were civilized, possessed consciousness and the ability to communicate, in which they hunted with weapons and were capable of horticulture. Then, according to the myths, the separation occurred. How? By way of the skin.

The non-humans simply changed costume.

Apart from their outer skin of hair, feathers or scales, the non-humans haven't really changed, say the myths. They're disguised humans, such as the following individual in New Guinea who appears in the skin of a pig, mentioned in a text cited by Descola.

Since he was coming from a very long way off, he travelled in the form of a pig, but at the entrance to the village he transformed himself once again into a man. First of all, he took off his skin and, since he was a man, he cut it up into a loincloth of fine leather. Around his neck, he hung a *ganda* buccal ornament which he assembled from pig's teeth. He attached his snout to a handle and made it into a club; his hairs were transformed into feathery adornments which he tied onto his head. His shield he made with his own ribs, still covered with their leather.

Non-humans don't appear very often without their disguises. The Achuar hunter stalks his prey with the knowledge he has acquired for that form of hunting, and at the same time murmurs incantations aimed at maintaining the link between the game animal and himself: he begs it to allow itself to be slaughtered, promising that it will be celebrated and the world will be repopulated with another 'itself'.

The real opportunities for meeting are the visits animals or plants make to humans in their dreams and, conversely, the visits the shaman makes to them in his trance. In both cases, each gets 'under the skin' of the other, says Descola, emphasizing 'under the skin'.

This is also what our lovers say when the *coup de foudre* of 'love at first sight' has struck. The other has got 'under their skin'.

The *coup de foudre*—our preferred form of trance—might be said, then, to be shamanic. This might be the sense of the expression 'the beast with two backs', when the composite animal—the beast—cancels out two human beings for as long as their sexual eclipse requires —that out-of-subjectivity experience in which each party loses consciousness.

To change into a quadruped, as Yvain did to recover his Laudine, was right for a knight who'd broken his word. To transform herself into a cat meowing at the end of a branch was right for a hunchbacked prioress who hadn't chosen to become a nun. To change into a jaguar was right for the dog Makanch which didn't want to hunt, and right for the ethnologist who was well disposed towards her.

And perhaps it's a better world, this world of the trance—this brief, tremulous moment that transforms both the human being and the dog into a jaguar and changes life—the life of the animal too.

Can we live without trances?

French law treats the endangering of another's life as an offence. The precautionary principle, which figures in the Constitution, seems to determine the rules of communal life. At the slightest shock, or when faced with any kind of ordeal, we hastily set up a psychological unit, whose aim, by lending an understanding ear, is to limit the danger or even render it intangible. The fear-based disciplines are regarded as barbaric. It doesn't take long to see the outcome, with young people engaging in uncontrolled, 'wildcat' eclipses, putting themselves in danger as they 'get their kicks'.

Who picks up the pieces afterwards? The ambulance service, the police and 'counsellors', that new orthopaedic entity whose aim is a return to the social norm. Who talks to the young about their trances? About their transformations? Their metamorphoses?

Though in our age the trance animal metabolizes on the silver screen into fictions emanating from the Anglo-Saxon world, it continues to appear among us in little groups that unconsciously perpetuate initiation rites, allowing amazing spirits—or 'amazing' people—to take possession of them on a regular basis.

When it isn't groups but individuals that are affected, they're called the mad or the 'mentally ill' and are cared for as such. With medication, confinement in hospitals, release and return—an in-and-out life, a life with eclipses.

The Art of the New

In 1950, in an introduction to the work of the great French ethnologist Marcel Mauss, Lévi-Strauss reflects on individual pathological behaviour. It's a key text, a magnificent piece of writing and one of those the mind returns to as to a fountainhead—particularly today.

For Lévi-Strauss, 'normal' behaviour fits with the symbolism structuring a society. By contrast, pathological—and hence 'abnormal'—behaviour attests to a purely individual symbolism that finds no place for itself in the social body. The abnormal is disturbing—that's its definition. In the short term—we shall see why passing time can change the nature of a state of delirium or madness—this individual symbolism isn't assimilable.

However, Lévi-Strauss tells us, no society can offer all its members the same degree of participation in 'the building of a symbolic structure which is only realizable (in the context of normal thinking) in the dimension of social life'. Every society has, then, its hard core of mad people.

He then takes the crucial step:

[S]trictly speaking, the person whom we call sane is the one who is capable of alienating himself, since he consents to an existence in a world definable only by the self-other relationship. The saneness of the individual mind implies participation in social life, just as the refusal to enter into it (but most importantly, the refusal to do so in the ways that it imposes) corresponds to the onset of mental disturbance.

It is duly acknowledged then—normal people are alienated. And what about the others, the unassimilable?

These rebels against the norms of social life have everywhere a function. It falls to them 'figuratively [to] represent certain forms of compromise which are not realisable on the collective plane', to 'simulate imaginary transitions, embody incompatible syntheses'. Let's take a close look at these propositions.

Whether it begins with feigning or is immediate, the trance offers 'imaginary transitions'. In the being-one of the *coup de foudre*, in animal metamorphosis or in the manifestation of a proprietary god, the trance drives a way through, changes skin, changes life.

And, as for these 'incompatible syntheses' or 'forms of compromise which are not realizable on the collective plane', we've seen some of them become compatible with social life before our very eyes. This is true of the shamanic gender changes but it's true also of sexual reassignments which have now become possible within our world and have been realized on the collective plane when they previously seemed unrealizable. What was in the past treated as a mental anomaly has become part of the norm and doesn't rank as pathology any more.

Might those who couldn't be made to conform to the norm actually be prophetic? Do what are, at one point, their 'incompatible syntheses' prefigure the time when they'll become compatible? It's not impossible.

This can't be examined without reflection on the function of language.

For Mauss and Lévi-Strauss there is in the language of every society a reserve pregnant with future meanings that is at the disposal of the mythmakers, the poets and those afflicted with disturbances incompatible with social life. This reserve is a place where words float around that are meaningless but will acquire meaning thanks to the world's mad, its poets and its outcasts.

Defining the healing effects of language on the body—effects he terms 'symbolic efficacy'—Lévi-Strauss describes its capacity to pass around the levels of a building comprising first the neuronal underpinnings, then the familial and social determinations making up the Unconscious, then the Conscious and, ultimately, as a last level, the power for change of the poet with new words at his disposal.

And he quotes Rimbaud's phrase about 'changing life', to which he says a loud yes.

These mythmakers, these inassimilable poets, these rebels, particularly the young ones, the possessed of yesteryear, marginal individuals from worlds whose norms are incompatible with our own, disturbing nomads with their own rules—they are thrown out, expelled or, alternatively, locked up. In our country, in what are especially tough times for those who will not compromise, we find them in prison. Away with them! Law and order. Security.

But since no society is ever integrally symbolic, these people with their symbolism that won't be integrated aren't content merely to spread disorder. Think of the strange destiny of the terrifying deliria of the Convulsionaries, pregnant with prophecies and revolution. They weren't just disturbing, those people (people whom others tried to cure and bring back into line by depriving them of their trances, because trances were abnormal)— they foreshadowed something.

What that was you can hear in rock music and rap. You can see it in raves, sense it in the spontaneous mass gatherings made possible by the Net and the mobile phone. You can divine a powerful desire for a new collectiveness beyond the scope of the present community.

Through what medium do the forms run that are going to bring change? Through *them*, through their eclipses from life.

If they eclipse themselves, it's because they aren't content with the social life we offer them. We, the sane, ordered and integrated, are, in their eyes, the alienated ones—the insane. For want of hope, these 'eclipsed' individuals invent transitions that shock us, syntheses incompatible with ourselves at the present time. Later on, we accept them. The new becomes normal.

They will invent others. They have a knack for the new.

A new that is vexing because it hasn't been seen before reinvents old patterns, transforms them and no longer jibes with the norm which, as one decade passes into the next, is soon outdated.

And I see in this the desire for the trance which, in the blink of an eye—in a lightning flash—enables life to be changed.

Bibliographical Note

CHANGING LIFE

ROUGET, Gilbert. *Music and Trance: A Theory of the Relations between Music and Possession*. Chicago and London: University of Chicago Press, 1985[1980].

Since its publication, I have taken this book with me everywhere I have travelled; it is a genuine guide to trances across the world. When, in 1996, I arrived in Senegal for a three-year stay, I reread Rouget, and that is how I came to know this ritual—the *ndöp*—which is specific to the Lebu of the Dakar region and, in other forms, to the Wolof of Senegal.

The undisputed expert on the *ndöp* is the anthropologist Andras Zempléni, the author of many articles published in the journal *Psychopathologie africaine*.

LEIRIS, Michel. *L'Afrique fantôme: De Dakar à Djibouti, 1931–33*. Paris: Gallimard, 1934.

———. 'La croyance aux génies zâr en Éthiopie du Nord' in Jean Jamin (ed.), *Miroir de l'Afrique*. Paris: Gallimard 'Quarto', 1996, pp. 925–45.

CHAPTER 1: THE *COUP DE FOUDRE*

LÉVI-STRAUSS, Claude. 'Finale' in *The Naked Man: Mythologiques*, VOL. 4 (John and Doreen Weightman trans). Chicago: University of Chicago Press, 1990[1971], pp. 625–95.

This fourth and last volume of *Mythologiques* ends with a long reflection on the effects of music, in which we find this marvellous statement on joy in music.

——. *Tristan et Yseut*. Paris: Gallimard 'Pléiade', 1994.

——. *Le Livre du Graal* (Daniel Poirion and Philippe Walter eds). 3 VOLS. Paris: Gallimard 'Pléiade', 2009.

DE TROYES, Chrétien. *Œuvres complètes* (Daniel Poirion ed.). Paris: Gallimard 'Pléiade', 1994.

RÉGNIER-BOHLER, Danielle (ed.). *La Légende arthurienne, Le Graal et la Table Ronde*. Paris: Robert Laffont 'Bouquins', 1997.

BÉGUIN, Albert, and Yves Bonnefoy (eds). *La Quête du Graal*. Paris: Éditions du Seuil 'Sagesses', 1965.

MARX, Jean. *La Légende arthurienne et le Graal*. Geneva: Slatkine, 1996[1952].

DELAY, Florence, and Jacques Roubaud. *Graal Théâtre*. Paris: Gallimard, 2005.

KÖHLER, Erich. *L'Aventure chevaleresque, idéal et réalité dans le roman courtois*. Paris: Gallimard 'Bibliothèque des Idées', 1974.

CHAPTER 2: THREE DROPS OF BLOOD

DE TROYES, Chrétien. 'Perceval le Gallois' in *Œuvres complètes* (Daniel Poirion ed.). Paris: Gallimard 'Pléiade', 1994, pp. 827–8.

On Oedipus and Perceval

LÉVI-STRAUSS, Claude. 'From Chrétien de Troyes to Richard Wagner' in *The View from Afar* (Joachim Neugros trans.). Oxford: Blackwell, 1985, pp. 219–34.

The first version of this text was written for the 1975 Bayreuth Festival programme.

CHAPTER 3: FILTH

ISAACSON, Rupert. *The Horse Boy*. London: Penguin, 2010.

CHAPTER 4: RUTTING REINDEER

HAMAYON, Roberte. *La Chasse à l'âme: Esquisse d'une théorie du chamanisme sibérien*. Nanterre: Société d'ethnologie, 1990.

LEIRIS, Michel. *L'Afrique fantôme: De Dakar à Djibouti, 1931–33*. Paris: Gallimard, 1934.

HELL, Bertrand. 'Négocier avec les esprits tromba à Mayotte: Retour sur le "théâtre vécu" de la possession'. *Gradhiva* 7 (nouvelle série) (2008): 20–1.

MÉTRAUX, Alfred. *Voodoo in Haiti*. New York: Schocken Books, 1972.

On Quesalid

LÉVI-STRAUSS, Claude. 'Part Three: Magic and Religion' in *Structural Anthropology* (Claire Jacobson and Brooke Schoepf trans). London: Penguin, 1972, pp. 165–241.

CHAPTER 5: CATS ON THE ENDS OF BRANCHES (POITOU-CHARENTES)

BARBIER, Charles. *Urbain Grandier et les possédées de Loudun*. Paris: Librairie d'art de Ludovic Baschet, 1880.

DE CERTEAU, Michel (ed.). *La Possession de Loudun*. Paris: Julliard, 1970.

MANDROU, Robert. *Possession et sorcellerie au XVIIIᵉ siècle*. Paris: Fayard, 1979.

On Adolf Hitler's Voice

KARPF, Anne. *La Voix, un univers invisible*. Paris: Autrement, 2008.

On Joey Starr

SORMAN, Joy. *Du bruit*. Paris: Gallimard, 2005.

CHAPTER 6: A-E-I-O-U
(PARIS AND OUTREAU, NORTHERN FRANCE)

MANDROU, Robert. *Magistrats et sorciers en France au XVIIe siècle: Une analyse de psychologie historique*. Paris: Plon, 1968.

WIEL, Dominique, and Lionel Duroy. *Que Dieu ait pitié de nous*. Paris: Oh! Éditions, 2006.

MAIRE, Catherine-Laurence (ed.). *Les Convulsionnaires de Saint-Médard: Miracles convulsions et prophéties à Paris au XVIIIe siècle*. Paris: Julliard, 1985.

VIDAL, Daniel. *Miracles et convulsions jansénistes au XVIIIe siècle: Le mal et sa connaissance*. Paris: PUF, 1987.

———. 'Une convulsionnaire janséniste au XIXe siècle' in Didier Michaux (ed.), *La Transe et l'hypnose*. Paris: Imago, 1995, pp. 105–19.

On Sati

WEINBERGER-THOMAS, Catherine. *Cendres d'immortalité*. Paris: Éditions du Seuil, 1996.

CHAPTER 7: THE LITTLE ANIMAL

BREUER, Josef, and Sigmund Freud. *Penguin Freud Library*, VOL. 3, *Studies on Hysteria* (J. and A. Strachey trans). London: Pelican, 1974.

RODRIGUÉ, Emilio. *Freud: Le siècle de la psychanalyse*, VOL. 1. Paris: Payot, 1996.

CHAPTER 8: DRACULA'S DAUGHTERS (IRELAND;USA)

STOKER, Bram. *Dracula*. London: Oxford University Press, 1992[1897].

MEYER, Stephenie. *Twilight*. New York: Little, Brown and Company, 2005.

——. *New Moon*. New York: Little, Brown and Company, 2006.

——. *Eclipse*. New York: Little, Brown and Company, 2007.

——. *Breaking Dawn*. New York: Little, Brown and Company, 2008.

CHAPTER 9: THE *TARANTATI* OF APULIA (SOUTHERN ITALY)

DE MARTINO, Ernesto. *The Land of Remorse*: *A Study of Southern Italian Tarantism* (Dorothy Louise Zinn trans.). London: Free Association Books, 2005[1961].

CHAPTER 10: THE BELLOWER (THE LOIRE)

FREYBURGER-GALLAND, Marie-Laure, Gérard Freyburger and Jean-Christian Tautil. *Sectes religieuses en Grèce et à Rome dans l'Antiquité païenne*. Paris: Les Belles Lettres, 1986.

DETIENNE, Marcel. *Dionysos at Large* (Arthur Goldhammer trans.). Cambridge, MA: Harvard University Press, 1989.

CHAPTER 11: MADONNA ORIENTE AND THE ANIMAL OF ECSTASY

GINZBURG, Carlo. *The Night Battles*: *Witchcraft and Agrarian Cults in the Sixteenth and Seventeenth Centuries* (John and Anne Tedeschi trans). Baltimore, MD: Johns Hopkins University Press, 1992[1966].

——. *Ecstasies. Deciphering the Witches' Sabbath* (Raymond Rosenthal trans.). Chicago: University of Chicago Press, 1991[1989].

On Father Christmas and dead children

LÉVI-STRAUSS, Claude. *Le Père Noël supplicié*. Pin-Balma: Sables, 1994.

CHAPTER 12: TRANS

SALADIN D'ANGLURE, Bernard. *Être et renaître inuit, homme, femme ou chamane*. Paris: Gallimard, 2006.

HAMAYON, Roberte. *La Chasse à l'âme: Esquisse d'une théorie du chamanisme sibérien*. Nanterre: Société d'ethnologie, 1990.

CHAPTER 13: DSMIII@SORCERY.ORG (USA;CANADA)

MULHERN, Sherill. 'L'hypnose, la mémoire et la déconstruction du moi post-moderne' in Didier Michaux (ed.), *La Transe et l'hypnose*. Paris: Imago, 1995.

CLÉMENT, Catherine. *Les Révolutions de l'inconscient, histoire et géographie des maladies de l'âme*. Paris: Éditions de La Martinière, 2001.

CHAPTER 14: WHEN THE BODY GOES INTO ECLIPSE
INSTEAD OF THE MIND

RAIMBAULT, Ginette, and Caroline Eliacheff. *Les Indomptables: Figures de l'anorexie*. Paris: Éditions du Seuil 'Points', 1989.

VERNANT, Jean-Pierre. 'Corps obscur, corps éclatant' in Charles Malamoud and Jean-Pierre Vernant (eds), *Le temps de la réflexion*. Paris: Gallimard, 1986, pp. 19–45.

On Elizabeth of Austria

CLÉMENT, Catherine. *Sissi, l'Impératrice anarchiste*. Paris: Gallimard, 1992.

HAMANN, Brigitte (ed.). *Kaiserin Elisabeth—Das poetische Tagebuch*. Vienna: Akademie der Wissenschaften, 1997.

CHAPTER 15: GATEWAYS TO THE BODY

SARADANANDA, Swami. *Sri Ramakrishna the Great Master* (Swami Jagadananda trans.). Chennai: Vedanta, 1979.

ROLLAND, Romain. *La Vie de Ramakrishna.* Paris: Robert Laffont, 1973[1929].

KAKAR, Sudhir, and Catherine Clément. *La Folle et le Saint.* Paris: Éditions du Seuil, 1993.

THOMAS, Louis-Vincent. *Le Cadavre.* Brussels: Éditions Complexe, 1980.

HAMAYON, Roberte. *La Chasse à l'âme: Esquisse d'une théorie du chamanisme sibérien.* Nanterre: Société d'ethnologie, 1990.

CLAUDEL, Paul. *The Satin Slipper: Or, The Worst is Not the Surest* (John O'Connor trans.). London: Yale University Press, 1931[1929].

SCHOTT-BILLMANN, France. 'Mémoire d'une religion universelle: La danse sur le feu en Grèce moderne' in France Schott-Billmann (ed.), *Danse et spiritualité.* Paris: Éditions Noesis, 1999, pp. 99–132.

GINZBURG, Carlo. *Ecstasies: Deciphering the Witches' Sabbath* (Raymond Rosenthal trans.). Chicago: University of Chicago Press, 1991[1989].

MARSAULT, Ralf. *Résistance à l'effacement.* Dijon: Les Presses du réel, 2010.

MURRAY, Margaret. *The God of the Witches.* Sioux Falls: NuVision Publications, 2005.

CHAPTER 16: DISCIPLINES OF FEAR

NATHAN, Tobie. *L'Influence qui guérit.* Paris: Odile Jacob, 1994.

BASTIDE, Roger. *Le Candomblé de Bahia.* Paris: Plon, 2000.

MARSAULT, Ralf. *Résistance à l'effacement*. Dijon: Les Presses du réel, 2010.

MEYER, Stephenie. *Twilight*. New York: Little, Brown and Company, 2005.

——. *New Moon*. New York: Little, Brown and Company, 2006.

——. *Eclipse*. New York: Little, Brown and Company, 2007.

——. *Breaking Dawn*. New York: Little, Brown and Company, 2008.

MOREIRA, Paul, and Hubert Prolongeau. *Travailler à en mourir*. Paris: Flammarion, 2009.

FREUD, Sigmund. 'Civilization and Its Discontents' in *Penguin Freud Library*, VOL. 12, *Civilization, Society and Religion* (J. Strachey trans.). London: Penguin, 1991[1930], pp. 251–340.

DESCOLA, Philippe. *The Spears of Twilight*: *Life and Death in the Amazon Jungle* (Janet Lloyd trans.). London: Flamingo, 1997[1993].

——. *Beyond Nature and Culture* (Janet Lloyd trans.). Chicago: University of Chicago Press, 2013[2005].

THE ART OF THE NEW

LÉVI-STRAUSS, Claude. *Introduction to the Work of Marcel Mauss* (Felicity Baker trans.). London: Routledge, 2001[1950].

——. 'Part Three: Magic and Religion' in *Structural Anthropology* (Claire Jacobson and Brooke Schoepf trans). London: Penguin, 1972, pp. 165–241.

And throughout, Gilbert Rouget, *Music and Trance*: *A Theory of the Relations between Music and Possession*. Chicago and London: University of Chicago Press, 1985[1980].

Index

Historical Figures

Quotation marks indicate the names of patients that were changed by their therapists for purposes of publication.

Mythic Figures

This category includes characters
in fiction and artist's pseudonyms.

GEOGRAPHICAL INDEX

Italics indicate groups or tribes.